Key
United
Methodist
Beliefs

Key
United
Methodist
Beliefs

William J. Abraham
David F. Watson

Abingdon Press
Nashville

KEY UNITED METHODIST BELIEFS

Copyright © 2013 by Abingdon Press

This book is printed on acid-free paper.

Library of Congress Cataloging-in-Publication Data

Abraham, William J. (William James), 1947-
  Key United Methodist Beliefs / William J. Abraham, David F. Watson.
    pages cm
  Includes bibliographical references and index.
  ISBN 978-1-4267-5661-0 (book - pbk. / trade pbk. : alk. paper)
1. United Methodist Church (U.S.)—Doctrines. 2. Methodist
Church—Doctrines. 3. Wesleyan Church—Doctrines.
I. Watson, David F., 1970- II. Title.
  BX8331.3.A27 2013
  230'.76—dc23

                                                                    2012050018

13 14 15 16 17 18 19 20 21 22—10 9 8 7 6 5 4 3 2 1

MANUFACTURED IN THE UNITED STATES OF AMERICA

Contents

Acknowledgments

We would like to thank a number of people who have assisted in the writing of this book. Casey Irwin has provided considerable help as a research assistant. We are grateful to Kathy Armistead for seeing the potential of this project. Jason Vickers helped in several conversations to refine some of the ideas we have presented here. Phyllis Ennist and Harriet Watson provided helpful feedback with regard to the book's accessibility and readability. Wendy Deichmann has been a strong source of encouragement for the writing of this book, and Sarah Blair provided considerable assistance in identifying a great many catechisms that we read in the early stages of conceptual planning.

To the members of First Light and In His Steps Sunday school classes in Highland Park United Methodist Church, Dallas, Texas.—WJA

For Luke, who has a kind and loving heart that shows the Holy Spirit's work in his life.

Introduction

Belief matters.

What we believe about God, about God's saving work within creation, about human wrongdoing, about the goal of our lives and our eternal destiny all matter. They make a difference with regard to how we think about ourselves and other people, about life and death, what we should value in life, and what kind of person we should hope to become. It is common to hear people talk about beliefs as if one is simply as good as another. For some, the one great sin is to insist on a clear difference between truth and falsehood, between right and wrong, but this perspective cannot coexist with Christianity. For that matter, it cannot coexist with Judaism or Islam, either, but that is not our topic here. The claims that we Christians make about what God has done for us—for all creation—in and through Jesus Christ really do matter.

Think about what Christians claim. The God of all creation loves us, even in the midst of all human wrongdoing. Because of this divine love, God became a human being in the person of Jesus Christ. Jesus lived a sinless life. He taught us how to live. He showed perfect love and called each person to the same kind of love, and in response to Jesus' teaching and example, human beings killed him. When he died, he took upon himself all of our wrongdoing, though he himself was blameless, and he offers us the opportunity now to be restored to a proper, loving relationship with God. Death, of course, was not the end for Jesus, for after three days he rose from the dead. Just as he rose from the dead and will live eternally, those who love and follow him will rise from the dead to eternal life.

That seems pretty important (to say the least), and yet so often in the church we neglect to teach these basic truths of the faith. It is so easy to focus on things like ways to live a more fulfilled life, the necessity of righting social wrongs, or becoming a better (fill in the blank). In many cases these things are truly important. Within Christianity, however, they make no sense outside of the context of what God has done for us in Jesus Christ and continues to do for us through the work of the Holy Spirit. Only God can truly change us. Only God can truly make us happy. Only God can give us eternal life.

God laments in the book of Hosea, "My people are destroyed for lack of knowledge" (4:6).[1] The more things change, the more they stay the same. In places where Christianity once thrived many people, even many of those who attend church, do not know the basic content of the Christian faith. Christianity, however, has always been about the good news: God loves us and has acted decisively to offer us new life, both now and forever. Without this good news, and the various ways in which Christians have filled out the details through the centuries, we cannot form new Christians. We can form churchgoers, but we cannot form Christians. Christianity has a basic content, and that content matters.

What we have written in these pages is not particularly new. This book is simply an account of the basic ideas of Christian faith, from a distinctive Wesleyan perspective. We have not provided an exhaustive account of the Christian faith, nor is this the only valid account of what Christians believe. It is a Wesleyan account, meaning that it is basic Christian belief shaped by the particular insights and emphases of John Wesley and like-minded Christians who have followed him. John, along with his brother Charles, led a powerful Christian renewal movement in England during the eighteenth century, a movement that continues to this very day, though often in highly institutionalized forms. The Wesleys emphasized that God acts within us to enable us to become more Christlike people. They thought of salvation not just as something confined to the future, but as present reality that continues into eternity. They were quite controversial in their own day, and if their descendants in the faith are less controversial today, perhaps it is because we have retained the form of our religion without its conviction, power, and passion. The truth is that we have also lost the intellectual content of the Christian faith.

Various kinds of Methodists, Nazarenes, the Wesleyan denomination, Church of God denominations, and other traditions fall into the broad category of "Wesleyanism." Many Pentecostals are also descendants of Wesley, since Pentecostalism came out of the Holiness movement, which came out of the Wesleyan movement. If you are reading this book and are attending a church in this tradition, we hope you find this account of the faith helpful. If you are of another tradition, we welcome you into this conversation. If you do not know what you believe or have no faith tradition, our prayer is that the words of these pages will lead you to know God in such a way that your life will never be the same.

The first nine chapters of this book are divided into five sections: "A Wesleyan Faith," "A Lived Faith," "A Deeper Faith," "The Catechism," and "In Your Own Words." The first section, "A Wesleyan Faith," is simply an account of the basic ideas under discussion, understood in light of some of John Wesley's theological insights. "A Lived Faith" discusses the practical implications of these ideas for Christian living. "A Deeper Faith" delves into some of the more difficult ideas of Christian thinking. "The Catechism" is a shorthand way of learning the basics of Wesleyan Christianity. Catechisms have long been a part of Christian faith, and we have read through many of them in the process of writing this book. The most significant for our purposes is found in the *Book of Common Prayer*, a work to which Wesley himself was deeply indebted. Up until about the second half of the twentieth century, Wesleyans produced catechisms on a regular basis. This stopped at about the same time that many Wesleyans began to render what we might call various forms of "revisionist" theology. The traditional way of writing catechisms has been in question-and-answer format, and we have kept that format here. The final section of each chapter, "In Your Own Words," includes study questions to help readers work through the ideas therein and integrate these ideas into their lives.

Right belief by itself, of course, is not enough. As Wesley put it, a person may be "as orthodox as the devil . . . and may all the while be as great a stranger as he to the religion of the heart."[2] Right belief does matter, though, because it helps us know God more fully, and it is by knowing and loving God, and by God's knowing and loving us, that we become the people God wants us to be. We read in the Roman Catholic catechism, "The whole concern of doctrine and its teaching must be directed to the love that never ends. Whether something is proposed for belief, for hope or for action, the love of our Lord must always be made accessible, so that anyone can see that all the works of perfect Christian virtue spring from love and have no other objective than to arrive at love."[3] The goal is love, and God is love. We should do all we can, therefore, to know God.

1 Who Is God the Father?

A Wesleyan Faith

When John Wesley set out to reform the nation and to spread scriptural holiness across England, he was fortunate to have a strong set of theological tailwinds driving him forward. He lived in a world that was saturated with the basic beliefs of Christianity. He studied and taught at the University of Oxford, where every teacher was required to assent to the core beliefs of the Church of England. He was a priest in a church in which all church members confessed every Sunday the faith of the ancient Church. He was the subject of a political state where only Christians who assented to one very important Christian belief, the doctrine of the Trinity, could serve in government. Even the calendar used by everyone was built around the Christian year, so that the great festivals of the Church were a constant reminder of the faith hammered out in the ancient Church. Hence Wesley did not need to worry very much about passing on the faith of the ages. He could take for granted that people were familiar with it. It was already deeply embedded in the minds of the people he sought to reach with the gospel. This does not mean, however, that they took it to heart, or that it was somehow life changing for them. Wesley's task was that of bringing folk into a living relationship with God the Father, through the revelation and work of the Son, in the power of the Holy Spirit. This was his passion.

Those theological tailwinds are no longer blowing across our culture today. Hence one of the first tasks is to be crystal clear about the identity of the God who Christians gladly serve and worship. The God of Christian faith, whether for Wesleyans or otherwise, is the Holy Trinity. The notion of the Trinity is hard to grasp, but it is at the core of what it means to love and serve the God who has saved us through Jesus Christ, and who lives with us every day by the power and work of the Holy Spirit. One of the most helpful discussions of the Trinity comes from a remarkable layperson, C. S. Lewis. In his book *Mere Christianity*, Lewis writes about the God of Christian faith as "three-personal." He invites us to think about the difference between a straight line drawn on a piece of paper, a square drawn on a piece of paper, and a cube. The straight line is one-dimensional and quite simple. The square, which consists of four straight lines, is two-dimensional. A cube, however, which consists of six squares, is three-dimensional. Of course, the cube does consist of straight lines, but combines them in such a way as to create a complex object. As Lewis puts it, "As you advance to more real and more complicated levels, you do not leave behind you the things you found on the simpler levels: you still have them, but combined in new ways—in ways you could not imagine if you knew only the simpler levels."[1]

What does this have to do with the Trinity? Lewis says that we human beings exist on a rather simple level. One person equals one being. Two people are two separate beings. With God, however, things work differently. Personalities are combined in new ways, ways that we who do not live on God's level cannot truly understand. In God's dimension, "you find a being who is three Persons while remaining one Being, just as a cube is six squares while remaining one cube."[2] Lewis notes that we cannot fully understand a being like that, "just as, if we were so made that we perceived only two dimensions in space we could never properly imagine a cube. But we can get a sort of faint notion of it."[3] So the God of Christian faith is a personal God, just as we humans are personal beings. God, however, is personal in a much more complex way than we are. God is "three-personal."

Christians have long called the three persons of the Trinity "Father, Son, and Holy Spirit." God the Father, specifically, is the First Person of the Trinity. Why is the Father first? Imagine a river that divides into two separate streams in the form of a Y. The two branches of the river originate from the same source, just as the Son and the Holy Spirit originate from the Father. The Father sent the Son—Jesus Christ—into the world for our salvation, and the Father sent the Holy Spirit into the world to lead us into that salvation. Now here is where the analogy with the river breaks down: for the river to be like the Trinity, all three parts—the source and the two branches—would have to be eternal. No part existed before any other. Rivers do not work like that, but God does.

There are many places in the Bible where God is called "Father." This designation for God is more frequent in the New Testament, but it does occur in the Old Testament too. The people of Israel at times talked about God as the father of their people. In Psalm 103:13 God is likened to a compassionate father: "As a father has compassion for his children, / so the LORD has compassion for those who fear him." In Proverbs 3:12, God is likened to a loving but disciplining father: "For the LORD reproves the one he loves, / as a father the son in whom he delights." Isaiah 64:8 speaks of God as a father in the sense of God's having given life to Israel: "Yet, O LORD, you are our Father; / we are the clay, and you are our potter; / we are all the work of your hand." Malachi 2:10 speaks of God as the one father and creator of all Israel. Some passages, such as 2 Samuel 7:13 and Psalm 2:7, speak of God as the father of Israel's king. They do not mean that these kings were God's sons the way Jesus was God's Son. Rather, the idea is that upon the ascension of the king, he was adopted as God's son.

There are other Old Testament references as well, but the language of Father for God occurs much more frequently in the New Testament. Jesus uses this language quite often in the Gospels (Matthew, Mark, Luke, and John). There are several reasons for this. One is that, as we have seen, all of Israel could call God "Father," as God was the father of this people. Another is that Jesus was the Messiah, a term used for Israel's kings, and, as we noted, Israel thought of its kings as sons of God. The main reason, however, is found on the lips of the angel Gabriel, as he speaks to Mary, Jesus' mother: "The Holy Spirit will come upon you, and the power of the Most High will overshadow you; therefore the child to be born will be holy; he will be called Son of God" (Luke 1:35). Jesus was God's Son in a unique way, quite differently from the ways in which Israel or her kings could be called God's sons.

Nevertheless, Jesus taught his disciples to pray saying, "Our Father" (Matt 6:9). God is the Father of Jesus, and God is the Father of all who wish to love and serve God, though in a different way. In the Old Testament, Israel looked at God as its father. Now we who are Gentiles can be adopted into God's household and become children of God as well. In Ephesians, we read that those who follow Christ are adopted into God's household (Eph 1:5), and within this household there is "one body and one Spirit, just as you were called to the one hope of your calling, one Lord, one faith, one baptism, one God and Father of all, who is above all and through all and in all" (4:4-6). In Romans 8:15-17 we read perhaps the most moving statement of our adoption into God's household: "For you did not receive a spirit of slavery to fall back into fear, but you have received a spirit of adoption. When we cry, 'Abba! Father!' it is that very Spirit bearing witness with our spirit that we are children of God, and if children, then heirs, heirs of God and joint heirs with Christ" (see also Gal 4:4-7). When we are baptized as followers of Christ, then, it is like being adopted into the home in which God is the Father.

As we have seen, though, calling God "Father" involves more than just the way in which we name God. It involves a certain set of ideas about the ways in which the Father, Son, and Holy Spirit relate to one another. In the Gospel of John, Jesus tells us that the Father sent the Son into the world (8:16, 18, 43; 10:36). The Son knows and loves the Father, and the Father loves the Son (19:15, 17). Jesus said, "The Father and I are one" (10:30); "I am in the Father and the Father is in me" (14:11); and "If you know me, you will know my Father also" (14:7). Do you see the close—actually insepa-rable—relationship between the Father and the Son? Moreover, the Son draws us to the Father. As Jesus says, "You will know that I am in my Father, and you in me, and I in you" (14:20). Christ is alive within us, and through Christ we are drawn into the life of God. In other parts of John's Gospel, Jesus tells his disciples that he has asked the Father to send the Holy Spirit, who will remain with Jesus' fol-lowers forever (14:15, see also 15:26). Jesus is explicit that the Father will send the Holy Spirit in Jesus' name to continue to teach about the will of the Father even after Jesus has departed (John 14:26). The Father is, in a sense, the wellspring of the Trinity, a wellspring who has poured forth the Son and the Holy Spirit eternally. It is impor-tant to note here that the notion of God as Father is not beholden to human fatherhood, but rather the notion of human fatherhood is shown to us in the relationship between the Father and the Son.

At the heart of what it means to talk of God as Father is God's creating, generative nature. God the Father is the source of both love and life. From the Father come the Son and the Holy Spirit. Likewise, through the Father, Son, and Holy Spirit come all of creation, all of humankind, the people of Israel, the person of Jesus Christ, and the salvation that is ours in Christ. Nothing exists without God, and the fountain of all life is God the Father. Therefore, we might think of God the Father as most purely expressing God's self-giving nature. It is within the very nature of God to give both life and love.

A Lived Faith

The ways in which we think about God affect the ways in which we think about our lives as Christians. If we believe that God shows us what it means to be loving, just, merciful, and forgiving, these ways of thinking about God will shape how we should act. If we think of God as harsh and judgmental, we ourselves are likely to be harsh and judgmental. If we think of God as warlike, or peaceful, tolerant, forgiving, or in some other way, this will probably affect the ways in which we live. To think of God as God the Father is to believe that God loves all people and wishes to save us from sin and death. If "God so loved the world that he gave his only Son, so that everyone who believes in him may not perish but may have eternal life" (John 3:16), then we ourselves should be loving, self-giving people as well. Or, as the First Letter of John puts it, "Beloved, let us love one another, because love is from God; everyone who loves is born of God and knows God. Whoever does not love does not know God, for God is love" (1 John 4:7-8).

To give of ourselves is at the heart of the Christian life. How do we use our money? How do we use our time? Do we use them only for ourselves, or in ways that give life, love, and hope to other people? Women and men from all different walks of life can give of themselves. People have different gifts (1 Cor 12:4-11), and these gifts contribute in particular ways to building up God's kingdom. Some people are good listeners, some are great preachers, and some are good with their hands. Some Christians are great writers, great teachers of children, and outstanding models of parenting. Some Christians know how to use money in ways that contribute to God's work in the world, while others may be gifted to glorify God through music and art. The point is not exactly what your gift is, but that your attitude toward life is one of self-giving. The nature of God the Father is one of self-giving, and in like kind, we should give of ourselves to God and our neighbors as well.

A Deeper Faith

The language of God as Father is deeply meaningful for many Christians. It is a way for them to know and love God more fully. It is a way to relate to God and to remind us of how deeply God loves and cares for us. At the same time, some people have raised objections about the use of masculine language for God, and there are good reasons for asking these kinds of questions. After all, God is not really a male, right? Jesus was a man, but the Holy Trinity is neither male nor female. The word "Spirit" in Hebrew, *ruach*, is normally feminine, and in Greek, *pneuma*, is neuter (neither masculine nor feminine). Additionally, some Christians have asked whether talking about God only in masculine terms leads to our understanding women as secondary in importance to men.

The Bible does at times use feminine language for God. In the Old Testament particularly, a number of passages use motherly images for God. Several of these occur in the book of Isaiah. In Isaiah 42:14 God is said to cry out like a woman in labor. In Isaiah 46:1-4, we read about people who have to carry around statues of false gods on beasts of burden, but, rather than being carried, God carries Israel like a mother carries her child in the womb. In Isaiah 49:15 we read of a God who is like a mother nursing a child and as a pregnant woman. Likewise, in Isaiah 66:13 we read, "As a mother comforts her child, / so I [God] will comfort you." Other books of the Bible employ this kind of imagery as well. Numbers 11:12 describes God as a mother and an infant's nurse, and Deuteronomy 32:15 describes God as the mother who has given birth to Israel. References to God in feminine terms are less common in the New Testament, though Jesus compares himself to a mother hen who wishes to protect her young (Matt 23:37), and he talks about the beginning of God's new reign on the earth as being like "birth pangs" (Mark 13:8; Matt 24:8).

Of course, motherly images certainly do not represent the experience of all women, just as fatherly images do not represent the experience of all men. The point here is that the Bible does at times reference God in feminine terms. If the Bible uses feminine language for God, is there any reason that we cannot or should not use this language too? Feminine language for God can be helpful and appropriate, *so long as we are clear that the God we are talking about is the God of Israel, the God who became flesh in Jesus Christ for our salvation, and who lives and abides with us in the Holy Spirit.*

The point of our God-talk, indeed of all Christian theology worth reading, is to bring us closer to God. To talk about God as Father, Son, and Holy Spirit connects us with the ways in which Christians have thought about God's saving work through the centuries. God the Father sent the Son for our salvation, and God continues to work in our lives through the Holy Spirit. There is too much packed into this language, too much theology built up around it, too many theological works that use this language, simply to dispense with it. Again, it is deeply meaningful language for many people. Nevertheless, while it would be harmful to stop using this language, it may be helpful and appropriate at times to use other language for God, including feminine language.

The Catechism

The Nature of God

Q. Who is the God of all creation?

A. The God of all creation is the Holy Trinity.

> "In the beginning when God created the heavens and the earth, the earth was a formless void and darkness covered the face of the deep, while a wind from God swept over the face of the waters" (Gen 1:1).

> "All things came into being through him, and without him not one thing came into being" (John 1:3).

> "For in him all things in heaven and on earth were created, things visible and invisible, whether thrones or dominions or rulers or powers—all things have been created through him and for him. He himself is before all things, and in him all things hold together" (Col 1:16-17)

Q. What does it mean to say that God is the Trinity? A. It means that God is "three persons, of one substance, power, and eternity— the Father, the Son, and the Holy Spirit"[4]

> "Hear, O Israel: The Lord is our God, the Lord alone" (Deut 6:4).

> "Go therefore and make disciples of all nations, baptizing them in the name of the Father and of the Son and of the Holy Spirit" (Matt 28:19).

9

Q. Who are the three persons of the Trinity?

A. Christians have long known them as Father, Son, and Holy Spirit.

Q. Why is it important to know God as the Trinity?

A. Because God has acted through all three persons of the Trinity for our salvation.

Q. Are the three persons of the Holy Trinity equal to one another?

A. The three persons of the Holy Trinity are equal to one another because they are one and the same God.[5]

Q. How do the three persons of the Holy Trinity differ from one another?

A. The three persons of the Trinity differ from one another as follows:

 a. God the Father is neither begotten nor proceeding from any other person.

 b. God the Son from all eternity is begotten from the Father.

 c. God the Holy Spirit from all eternity proceeds from the Father.[6]

"When the Advocate comes, whom I will send to you from the Father, the Spirit of truth who comes from the Father, he will testify on my behalf." (John 15:26).

"And because you are children, God has sent the Spirit of his Son into our hearts, crying, 'Abba! Father!' " (Gal 4:6).

God the Father

Q. Who is God the Father?

A. The First Person of the Trinity, from whom the Son is eternally begotten, and from whom the Holy Spirit eternally proceeds.

In Your Own Words

1. Some people find the concept of God as Father valuable and enriching, while others struggle with it. Perhaps their relationship with their own father was difficult. How is God like and unlike your father?

2. Proverbs 3:12 says that God reproves, or disciplines, his children. When is a time in your life when you felt God disciplined you? In your opinion what are the most effective ways to discipline children? Do you practice spiritual disciplines (acts of mercy, fasting, reading the Scripture, partaking of the sacraments, attending worship, and so forth)?

3. What does the Lord's Prayer teach us about God our Father? How is understanding God as *our* Father different from understanding God only as *my* Father?

4. God is neither male nor female, but how can using female imagery enrich your own understanding of God?

5. God is our Creator who continues to work on our lives today. Share a time when you felt close to God. Where were you? Who were you with? Did it change you in any way?

2 Who Is God the Son?

A Wesleyan Faith

One of the most distinctive and beautiful portraits of John Wesley that comes down to us from the past places Wesley, dressed in the attire of an Anglican priest, standing beside a cross in a market square. Small of stature, he stands tall, holding a Bible in one hand; with the other hand extended in an arc in the air, he is clearly calling on those present to heed the invitation to accept the good news of salvation. A motley crew of humanity is gathered around him: old and young, male and female, rich and poor. In some versions even the local dogs have shown up to listen. This is Wesley at full stretch, engaged in one of the central acts of Christian ministry: preaching the gospel to those who are really hearing it for perhaps the very first time in their lives. His favorite phrase for describing what he was doing was, "I offered them Christ." This was not some cheap slogan, for Wesley meant that he offered Christ in all his offices, that is, as prophet, priest, and king. As prophet, Christ taught us truly about God; as priest, he made sacrifice for the sins of the whole world; and as king, he became Lord of all who put their faith in him. The neat summary of Christian belief concerning the person and work of Christ takes us directly to a pivotal element in any serious version of Christianity. We need to explore who Christ really is.

In the last chapter we talked about God as "three-personal." The First Person of the Trinity is God the Father, and the Second Person of the Trinity is God the Son. Christian thinkers through the centuries have written untold pages on the Son who comes forth from the Father, but the point of all of this high-flying theology is this: the Father sends the Son to save us from sin and death, so that we can live as God wants in this life, and so that we can live with God forever. The sending of the Son into the world is an act of divine love.

The people of Israel had always believed that God was at work in the world—through creation, by choosing Israel, by loving and chastening the nation, by giving the law, by the raising up of prophets, and in many, many other ways. The early Christians believed this too, though they also believed that God had acted most decisively in the life of one person: Jesus, whom they called the Messiah. The words *Messiah* and *Christ* mean the same thing. The first comes from Hebrew, the second from Greek, but both mean "anointed one." What does anointing have to do with anything? It was a way of designating a person whom God had chosen for a special service, specifically for leadership. The first priests of Israel, Aaron and his sons, were anointed by Moses as a way of inaugurating their priesthood (Exod 28:41). When Saul became the first king of Israel, the prophet Samuel poured oil over his head, kissed him, and said, "The LORD has anointed you ruler of his people Israel" (1 Sam 10:1). Likewise, when David became king following Saul, Samuel anointed him as well, "and the spirit of the LORD came mightily upon David from that day forward" (1 Sam 16:13). Even a Gentile, the Persian king Cyrus, is called God's anointed (Isa 45:51) because God chose him to accomplish divine purposes.

Jesus, like these other figures, is chosen to fulfill God's plans, but Jesus is chosen to do so not just for Israel, but also for the entire world. Jesus the Messiah is the one through whom God would bring salvation to all people. Jesus' work as the Messiah, however, plays out differently than that of other people specially chosen by God and anointed. Great prophets and leaders anointed Aaron and his sons, along with Saul and David. In the case of Aaron, it was Moses who anointed, and in the cases of Saul and David, it was Samuel. Jesus, however, was anointed by an unnamed woman in the house of someone named "Simon the leper" (Mark 14:3-9), and his anointing as the Messiah doubles as his anointing for burial (14:8). Jesus will save not only through his life, but also through his death on the cross. His role as the Messiah is inseparable from this salvation. While Jesus is the Messiah, then, he is a very different kind of messiah, one who is chosen to give of himself in service and humility, even to the point of his own death, so that people like us, people who have not always lived as God wished, can be restored to a proper relationship with God. (In chapter 6 we'll talk more about how Jesus restores our relationship with God.)

Jesus is different from other leaders of Israel in another way too: Jesus is the Son of God, not figuratively, but literally. Today, in the modern city of Nazareth in Israel, sits one of the most beautiful churches in the world. It is called the Basilica of the Annunciation. Within this church is an altar upon which are inscribed the Latin words, *verbum caro hic factum est*, which mean, "Here the Word became flesh." Whether or not this altar marks the exact spot where the event took place, the idea is clear: God became a particular person at a particular time and place. When Christians talk about the "Annunciation," we are talking about the angel Gabriel's words to the Virgin Mary found in Luke 1:26-38. Gabriel says to Mary that she will conceive, bear a son, and name him Jesus. He says, "He will be great, and will be called the Son of the Most High, and the Lord God will give to him the throne of his ancestor David" (1:32). Understandably, this confuses Mary. "How can this be, since I am a virgin?" she asks (1:34). Gabriel responds, "The Holy Spirit will come upon you, and the power of the Most High will overshadow you; therefore the child to be born will be holy; he will be called Son of God" (1:35). In other words, God—through the Holy Spirit—will be the father of this child. Presumably, Mary could respond with fear, refusal, or simply confusion, but instead she responds, "Here am I, the servant of the Lord; let it be with me according to your word" (1:38).

With that, the greatest miracle the world has ever known took place—the Incarnation. This term, *Incarnation*, describes what happened when God became a human being. By the power of the Holy Spirit, Jesus was conceived within Mary. Jesus was, in a very real way, the Son of God. Therefore within Jesus are both humanity and divinity. In Colossians 1:15-23, we find what is probably an ancient Christian hymn (though here it is not printed in verse). Some of the ideas most crucial to our understanding of the Incarnation are expressed in this passage:

> He is the image of the invisible God, the firstborn of all creation; for in him all things in heaven and on earth were created, things visible and invisible, whether thrones or dominions or rulers or powers—all things have been created through him and for him. He himself is before all things, and in him all things hold together. He is the head of the body, the church; he is the beginning, the firstborn from the dead, so that he might come to have first place in everything. For in him all the fullness of God was pleased to dwell, and through him God was pleased to reconcile to himself all things, whether on earth or in heaven, by making peace through the blood of his cross.

This passage of Scripture offers us a glimpse of Christ's divine nature—that Christ existed before all of creation, that he is the very image of God, and that the fullness of God dwelled within Christ.

Christ is here called the "firstborn from the dead," meaning that Christ's resurrection is the first, but not the last, because resurrection is not just for Jesus only, but for all who follow him. Moreover, it was through Christ that all of creation came into being. If we think about this in terms of the three-personal nature of God, we could say that God the Father is the wellspring of life, but it is through God the Son that creation actually came into being. We see similar ideas in John 1:3 and Hebrews 1:2. The Father is the source, but the Son is the creator.

Humanity and divinity are both fully present in Jesus Christ. Yet humanity and divinity are hard concepts to hold together. Early in the Church's history, Christians debated with one another over such questions as, "If Jesus was divine, did he have a real human body?" "Was Jesus an angel or a spirit, rather than a human being?" and "Was Jesus more divine than human, or more human than divine, or equally human and divine?" Over time, however, the Church came to this basic consensus: Jesus was fully divine and fully human. Yes, Jesus had a flesh-and-blood body. Yes, he suffered, and he really died. And, yes, he was also fully God.

One of the oldest bits of Christian worship we have is found in Paul's Letter to the Philippians. In this letter, Paul is dealing with arguments within the church in Philippi. He tells these Christians that they should shun selfish ambition and conceit and humble them-selves, even going so far as to regard other people as better than they are. He tells them that their example in this regard is Christ himself, and then he quotes from a song that these Christians sang together in worship. In Philippians 2:6-11, Paul says that Christ Jesus,

> though he was in the form of God,
>> did not regard equality with God
>> as something to be exploited,

but emptied himself,
    taking the form of a slave,
    being born in human likeness.
And being found in human form,
    he humbled himself
    and became obedient to the point of death—
    even death on a cross.
Therefore God also highly exalted him
    and gave him the name
    that is above every name,
so that at the name of Jesus
    every knee should bend,
    in heaven and on earth and under the earth,
and every tongue should confess
    that Jesus Christ is Lord,
    to the glory of God the Father.

This is sometimes called the *kenosis* hymn. *Kenosis* is a Greek word that means "emptying." This is a hymn about what it means for Christ to empty himself of his power and majesty, to become a human, to humble himself to the point of death—even death on a cross. Rather than seeking to hold on to the glory, power, and honor that were rightly his, he emptied himself of these, and he gave of himself for others. That is why God the Father exalted Jesus. God raised him from the dead, and the risen Christ lives eternally with the Father.

This is the heart of the Incarnation: in Jesus Christ, God took on the life of a human being. How can this be? Didn't Jesus pray to God? Didn't Jesus say things about his Father in heaven? How is it that Jesus could be God if God was also in heaven, receiving Jesus' prayers? The key to these questions is remembering that the Christian God is three-personal. God is Father, Son, and Holy Spirit.

God the Son became flesh in Jesus Christ, and while God the Father and the Holy Spirit were present with the Son, it was nonetheless through the Son that God took on humanity. When Jesus prayed, he prayed to God the Father. God's heavenly and spiritual reign continued while God the Son was made human in Jesus Christ.

The prologue to the Gospel of John (John 1:1-18) reflects yet another ancient hymn. In this hymn, Jesus is said to have come from God's Word. For both Jews and Gentiles in the ancient world, the Greek word *logos*—which we normally translate as "word"—had a wide range of meanings. To sum them up in the context of this hymn, though, when these early Christians talked of God's "Word," they meant to refer to God's will, ordering of the universe, reason, and power. It is through God's Word that life came into being. Indeed, through God's Word, everything came into being. Greek-speaking people in the first century would have been familiar with this notion of the "Word" as the creative agent of a divine being, the way we today are familiar with abstract concepts such as democracy, capitalism, and evolution. These concepts are just part of the sea in which we swim, as the "Word" was to ancient Greek-speaking people. For us living today, it can be hard to get our heads around the ancient concept of the Word because it is not part of our common chest of ideas. Nevertheless, it can be helpful to think of God's Word as God's self-expression. To put it differently, a sentence that you think in your head is different from a sentence you speak out loud. The sentence spoken out loud is like God's Word.

John, however, makes an astounding claim, one that did not match up with commonplace thinking about the Word: "the Word became flesh and lived among us." This was not how most ancient people thought about the Word. For these people, flesh and spirit were opposed to each other. They were like oil and water: you could put them in the same bowl, but they did not mix. The flesh was simply a poor replication of the spirit. God's Word was Spirit, yet these early Christians said that God's Word did become flesh. The Word did not put on flesh or simply have the appearance of flesh. The Word became flesh, and when that happened, Jesus Christ came into the world. Jesus is God's self-expression in the flesh. Christ came into the world to draw us closer to God.

Jesus, being fully human, had a real body, and he really did die. Yet death was not the end for Jesus—nor is death the end for those who love and follow Jesus. Jesus was raised from the dead. We call this the "Resurrection." On the third day after Jesus died, he rose from the dead. The Bible is clear that it was not Jesus' spirit, or ghost, that rose, but his body. Luke recounts one of Jesus' post-resurrection appearances, when he appeared to his disciples. He came to them and said,

> "Peace be with you." They were startled and terrified, and thought that they were seeing a ghost. He said to them, "Why are you frightened, and why do doubts arise in your hearts? Look at my hands and my feet; see that it is I myself. Touch me and see; for a ghost does not have flesh and bones as you see that I have."

As if to stress the point, Jesus asks them for something to eat. The disciples give Jesus a piece of fish, and he eats it in their presence (Luke 24:36-43). Likewise in John's Gospel, Jesus appears to his disciples and shows them the marks of the crucifixion in his hands and the mark from a Roman soldier's spear in his side (20:20). Thomas had the remarkably bad luck of being absent at this particular moment, and he told the other disciples, "Unless I see the mark of the nails in his hands, and put my finger in the mark of the nails and my hand in his side, I will not believe" (20:25). A week later, Thomas had this opportunity, after which he exclaimed, "My Lord and my God!" (20:28).

So Jesus, after his resurrection, has a real body. It is, however, a different kind of body than he had prior to the resurrection. Luke tells us that Jesus said that, in the resurrection, people cannot die anymore, "because they are like angels and are children of God" (20:36). John's Gospel tells that Jesus appeared to Mary Magdalene after his resurrection, but he told her, "Do not hold on to me, because I have not yet ascended to the Father" (20:17). John tells of Jesus appearing in a locked room (20:19). The Apostle Paul writes that after the resurrection Jesus appeared to more than five hundred people at one time (1 Cor 15:6). Paul also says, "What is sown [the mortal body] is perishable, what is raised is imperishable" (1 Cor 15:42), and he talks about the resurrected body as a "spiritual body." What happens in Jesus' resurrection, then, is not the resuscitation of a corpse, but a miracle of God whereby Christ receives a new, spiritual body, but a body nonetheless. Likewise, we who know and love Jesus will be raised up as he was, in a new, spiritual body, one that will never die.

A Lived Faith

Through Jesus Christ, God, who had all power, majesty, glory, and honor, took on human form. Christ did not come as a conquering general, a mighty ruler, or a wealthy captain of industry. Christ came as a common person. He worked with his hands. He ate common, everyday food and wore common, everyday clothes. He was not one of the power elite. Jesus says of himself in Mark 10:45, "For the Son of Man came not to be served but to serve, and to give his life a ransom for many." Christ had more power and more claim to glory than any of us could ever imagine, and he gave all of it up for people like us. Though we call him "Lord," he came to serve. He healed the sick, fed the hungry, cast out demons, and taught about God's will for humankind. He washed the feet of his own followers (John 13:1-20).

He did not ask for money or seek fame for doing these acts of kindness. He was not doing these things for himself, but for people in need: sick people, hurting people, people who needed to hear about God's will for their lives. Most significantly of all, Jesus died on the cross. Crucifixion was often called the "slave's punishment" in Jesus' day. It was generally considered the worst way to die. It was not only a form of physical torture, but it was also a way to humiliate and make an example of a criminal, a way to deter others from engaging in the kind of behavior of which the victim of crucifixion was accused. All of this takes us back to the notion of *kenosis,* or "emptying" (discussed above). Christ did not empty himself of his divinity, but he did empty himself of all of the privilege that went along with being God.

The Incarnation says something about the way in which God believes that human beings should live. Jesus lived in a particular way that teaches us about the virtues that we, his followers, should try to embody. Of course, none of us is Jesus, and we should not ever confuse ourselves with Jesus, but we can try to embody the same kind of virtues that Jesus embodied. Jesus, first and foremost, embodies self-giving. In fact, we might say that Jesus is God's self-giving to humankind. If God is self-giving in such a remarkable way, those who try to live as God would wish should be self-giving as well. Philippians tells us that Christ "humbled himself" in taking on human form. Therefore we who follow Christ should also try to embody the virtue of humility. Jesus' ministry was one of service to others through healing, teaching, and acts of love and kindness. Therefore we should also live lives in service to others in the ways that are available to us. Jesus welcomed people into his group who were thought to be undesirables by many in his day because they were sick, sinful, poor, or perhaps all three. We who follow Jesus, then, should welcome within our family of faith those who are outcast, hurting, desperate, and in need of grace and forgiveness.

In the light of the Incarnation, how should we relate to other people? How should we spend our money? How should we spend our time? To what extent can we describe our lives as self-giving? To what extent can we say that we embody humility? Within much of our culture, these are not the values that are held up before us. Rather, the values of personal gain, fame, wealth, advancement, and prestige are being held up before us all of the time. In a culture that is obsessed with celebrity, with reality TV, and with shows in which people routinely stab one another in the back in the hopes of winning both money and celebrity, the Incarnation challenges us at the deepest level to live in a way that is countercultural. If we view the world through the lens of the Incarnation, we will see these self-aggrandizing values for what they are: they are sinful.

A Deeper Faith

The claim that Jesus of Nazareth is fully human and fully divine is clearly a dramatic, even sensational, claim. We can all agree on its relevance, but can we really say it is true? What drove the early disciples and the early church to make such an amazing assertion?

Clearly, the first disciples were deeply puzzled by their experience of Jesus. Most if not all of them saw Jesus initially as a potential political figure who would liberate them from the hated Roman occupation and restore the fortunes of Israel as a nation. This fitted nicely with their own desires to be top dogs in the new regime they hoped Jesus would establish in Jerusalem. Over time, they came to see things differently. At one level this meant they had to reorder their own desires to align them with those of Jesus and face the suffering this would involve. However, only masochists would suffer for a cause that they found incredible. Hence at a deeper intellectual level they came around to seeing Jesus as the Savior who would liberate them not only from political oppression but also from bondage to sin and evil. Their Jewish heritage paved the way for this radical shift of vision by making it clear that God was indeed a liberator, but the liberation cut much deeper than mere liberation from political oppression. Human nature itself needed to be set free from its hopelessly disordered state and turned the right way up. Only God could pull off this deeper operation.

The key to the change of their vision of Jesus lay in the actions they saw Jesus perform. The bottom line was that Jesus performed the acts that every informed Jew knew only God could perform. When they saw Jesus teach with searching authority; when they witnessed him heal with direct miraculous power; when they heard him forgive sins against God without hesitation; when they saw him exercise direct power over sickness, nature, and death; when they noted his amazing authority over evil and the demonic; all these gave them an acute pain in the brain. Why? It was because these were exactly the acts that identified the very God of Israel. Moreover, in his trial, Jesus openly claimed to be the Son of God (see Mark 14:61-62). When you ponder these over time, you are left with few options. You can say that Jesus was an imposter and a fraud. You can answer that he needs psychiatric attention. Or you can begin to see that Jesus is indeed something much more than a mere prophet or teacher: he really is the Son of God. Once you make this shift, other things fall into place. Why is it that he never asks forgiveness for his own sins? How is it that there is such intimacy with the God of Israel? Why and how was he was so dramatically raised from the dead? Why and how does Jesus, risen from the dead, bestow on the first disciples and on us the Holy Spirit? Why does the early church begin to worship him as they worship the God of Israel? What happened is that Jesus came to be seen as the Lord, the Son of God, acting as God did to recreate and restore the world to sanity and good health.

Historians have always been baffled by Jesus. Over the last two hundred years, when many have rejected the teaching of the Church about Jesus, they have tried ever so hard to figure out an alternative. Try as they may, they cannot reach a consensus. In many cases they simply project their own vision of what they would like Jesus to be; they recreate Jesus in their own image. The early disciples did not do this. On the contrary, they were driven to abandon their image of Jesus and learn a whole new way of thinking and speaking about him. We can see this in the Gospels, most especially in the Gospel of John. The early church ran with this profound vision of Jesus as the Son of God and in time hammered out the full implications that we find written up so succinctly in the creeds. This kind of move involved an intellectual revolution in the theology of Judaism. It required intense reflection and amazing intellectual boldness. It also required a massive revolution in how they lived; and it led into blessings untold in their lives and in the church as a whole. The same holds true today. This is the faith that has sustained the saints and martyrs of history; it also sustains deep faith today, the kind of faith that can really change the world.

The Catechism

God the Son

Q. Who is God the Son?

A. The Second Person of the Trinity, through whom all creation has come into being. The Son is the only perfect image of the Father, and he shows us the nature of God.

> "In the beginning was the Word, and the Word was with God, and the Word was God. He was in the beginning with God. All things came into being through him, and without him not one thing came into being" (John 1:1-3).

Q. What is the nature of God revealed in Jesus?

A. God is love.[1]

"God is love" (1 John 4:8).

Q. What do we mean when we say that Jesus was conceived by the power of the Holy Spirit and became incarnate from the Virgin Mary?

A. We mean that by God's own act, his divine Son received our human nature from the Virgin Mary, his mother.[2]

> "Therefore the Lord himself will give you a sign. Look, the young woman is with child and shall bear a son, and shall name him Immanuel" (Isa 7:14).

> "The angel said to her, 'The Holy Spirit will come upon you, and the power of the Most High will overshadow you; therefore the child to be born will be holy; he will be called Son of God. . . . For nothing will be impossible with God'" (Luke 1:35, 37).

> "Now the birth of Jesus the Messiah took place in this way. When his mother Mary had been engaged to Joseph, but before they lived together, she was found to be with child from the Holy Spirit. Her husband Joseph, being a righteous man and unwilling to expose her to public disgrace, planned to dismiss her quietly. But just when he had resolved to do this, an angel of the Lord appeared to him in a dream and said,

'Joseph, son of David, do not be afraid to take Mary as your wife, for the child conceived in her is from the Holy Spirit. She will bear a son, and you are to name him Jesus, for he will save his people from their sins.' All this took place to fulfill what had been spoken by the Lord through the prophet:

'Look, the virgin shall conceive and bear a son,
and they shall name him Emmanuel,'

which means, 'God is with us.' When Joseph awoke from sleep, he did as the angel of the Lord commanded him; he took her as his wife, but had no marital relations with her until she had borne a son; and he named him Jesus" (Matt 1:18-25).

Q. Why did he take our human nature?

A. The divine Son became human so that in him human beings might be adopted as children of God, and be made heirs of God's kingdom.[3]

"But when the fullness of time had come, God sent his Son, born of a woman, born under the law, in order to redeem those who were under the law, so that we might receive adoption as children" (Gal 4:4-5).

"But to all who received him, who believed in his name, he gave power to become children of God" (John 1:12).

"He has rescued us from the power of darkness and transferred us into the kingdom of his beloved Son, in whom we have redemption, the forgiveness of sins" (Col 1:13-14).

"If I am delayed, you may know how one ought to behave in the household of God, which is the church of the living God, the pillar and bulwark of the truth" (1 Tim 3:15).

Q. What is the relationship between Jesus' divinity and his humanity?

A. Jesus is fully divine and fully human.

> "[Christ], though he was in the form of God,
>   did not regard equality with God
>   as something to be exploited,
> but emptied himself,
>   taking the form of a slave,
>   being born in human likeness" (Phil 2:6-7).

"He is the image of the invisible God, the firstborn of all creation" (Col 1:15).

"For in him the whole fullness of deity dwells bodily" (Col 2:9).

Q. What is the great importance of Jesus' suffering and death?

A. By his death, Christ made perfect redemption, propitiation, and satisfaction for all the sins of the whole world, both original and actual.[4]

> "Surely he has borne our infirmities
>   and carried our diseases;
> yet we accounted him stricken,

28

struck down by God, and afflicted.
But he was wounded for our transgressions,
    crushed for our iniquities;
upon him was the punishment that made us whole,
    and by his bruises we are healed" (Isa 53:4-5).

"The next day he saw Jesus coming toward him and declared, 'Here is the Lamb of God who takes away the sin of the world!'" (John 1:29).

"[He] was handed over to death for our trespasses and was raised for our justification" (Rom 4:25).

"God proves his love for us in that while we still were sinners Christ died for us" (Rom 5:8).

"For our sake he made him to be sin who knew no sin, so that in him we might become the righteousness of God" (2 Cor 5:21).

"Christ redeemed us from the curse of the law by becoming a curse for us—for it is written, 'Cursed is everyone who hangs on a tree'" (Gal 3:13).

"In him we have redemption through his blood, the forgiveness of our trespasses, according to the riches of his grace" (Eph 1:7).

"If we walk in the light as he himself is in the light, we have fellowship with one another, and the blood of Jesus his Son cleanses us from all sin" (1 John 1:7).

"He is the atoning sacrifice for our sins, and not for ours only but also for the sins of the whole world" (1 John 2:2).

Q. What is the great significance of Jesus' bodily resurrection?

A. In the Resurrection Jesus overcame death, and his rising presages our own.

"We know that Christ, being raised from the dead, will never die again; death no longer has dominion over him" (Rom 6:9).

"But in fact Christ has been raised from the dead, the first fruits of those who have died. For since death came through a human being, the resurrection of the dead has also come through a human being" (1 Cor 15:20-21).

"And he died for all, so that those who live might live no longer for themselves, but for him who died and was raised for them" (2 Cor 5:15).

Q. What does it mean to say that Jesus ascended into heaven?

A. We mean that Jesus took our human nature into heaven, where he now reigns with the Father and intercedes for us.[5]

"For / there is one God; / there is also one mediator between God and humankind, / Christ Jesus, himself human, / who gave himself a ransom for all / —this was attested at the right time" (1 Tim 2:5-6).

"[He] has gone into heaven and is at the right hand of God, with angels, authorities, and powers made subject to him" (1 Pet 3:22).

"My little children, I am writing these things to you so that you may not sin. But if anyone does sin, we have an advocate with the Father, Jesus Christ the righteous" (1 John 2:1).

Q. How can we share in his victory over sin, suffering, and death?[6]

A. We receive our salvation by putting our whole trust in Jesus Christ for our salvation.

"Jesus said to her, 'I am the resurrection and the life. Those who believe in me, even though they die, will live, and everyone who lives and believes in me will never die. Do you believe this?'" (John 11:25-26).

"Jesus said to him, 'Have I been with you all this time, Philip, and you still do not know me? Whoever has seen me has seen the Father'" (John 14:9).

"There is salvation in no one else, for there is no other name under heaven given among mortals by which we must be saved" (Acts 4:12).

In Christ God was reconciling the world to himself, not counting their trespasses against them, and entrusting the message of reconciliation to us" (2 Cor 5:19).

"So that at the name of Jesus
    every knee should bend,
    in heaven and on earth and under the earth,
and every tongue should confess
    that Jesus Christ is Lord,
    to the glory of God the Father" (Phil 2:10-11).

"He has now reconciled in his fleshly body through death, so as to present you holy and blameless and irreproachable before him" (Col 1:22).

"As you therefore have received Christ Jesus the Lord, continue to live your lives in him" (Col 2:6).

In Your Own Words

1. How did you become a Christian? Who offered you Christ? How do you offer Christ to others?

2. As the Messiah, Jesus is chosen to give of himself in service and humility and, as Christians, we are called to do the same thing. Give an example of how you serve. Whose service do you admire? In what ways does your church encourage people to serve?

3. There is a lot of talk about leadership these days—in the church, in business, in the community, in the home. What are the most important qualities of a leader? Is leadership something a person is born with or something that can be learned?

4. The Church has debated about the humanity and divinity of Christ for many years. How do you understand that Jesus was both human and divine? What difference does it make to say that Jesus is God? What difference does it make that Jesus lived and dwelt among us?

5. On the cross, Jesus emptied himself of all of his privileges. What privileges were you born with? What privileges were you born without? What do privileges do for a person? What does it say to you that Jesus would suffer and die on a cross?

6. What does it mean to you that Jesus forgives, heals, guides, sustains, and reconciles? Give an example of a time when you or someone you know experienced the love of Jesus as forgiveness, healing, guidance, or reconciliation.

3 Who Is God the Holy Spirit?

A Wesleyan Faith

When John Wesley wandered into a small fellowship meeting in Aldersgate, London, on May 24, 1738, he believed in the reality of the Holy Spirit, but he had only a second-hand notion of what it was to experience the Holy Spirit. When he left, he knew for the first time in his life what it was like to feel the inner working of the Holy Spirit in his own heart and soul. This was the beginning of a spiritual and theological revolution that continues to rattle around the Christian world, much to the consternation of many Christians even today. As a result of this experience of the Spirit, Wesley knew deep down that he was accepted and loved by God. He described this in biblical terms as the experience of the inner witness of the Holy Spirit (Rom 8:15-17). The image is a legal one. Witnesses tell of what they know firsthand. In court, they cannot present what they picked up by e-mail, or recycle the gossip they overheard at the local pub, or repeat the rumors they have heard at the airport. They must speak truthfully. It is exactly like this with the Holy Spirit, speaking in the heart and bearing witness that we really are children of God. God the Spirit is speaking straight from the heart and mind of God. For Wesley this was a profoundly invigorating moment. It set him at liberty in his relationship with God. To be sure, he found it

35

difficult to sort it all out intellectually. Over the next nine months and beyond he pondered how best to speak of what had happened. However, he now had direct experience of the Person of the Holy Spirit. The Spirit was no longer an abstract idea; the Spirit was a Person who was intimately at work in the human heart.

The Holy Spirit (in some older writings called the "Holy Ghost") is the Third Person of the three-personal God. The power and work of the Holy Spirit are at the center of what it means to be a Wesleyan. Jesus returned to God the Father after the Resurrection, but we are not alone in our lives as Christians. Rather, God is with us in the Person and work of the Holy Spirit. When we see Christians engage in great works of love and mercy, when people give their lives over to Christ, when someone we never thought would change suddenly embarks on a new kind of life, this is the work of the Holy Spirit. Various people may be skilled evangelists, calling people to give their lives to Christ, but change—real change—within the individual and within churches happens through the power and work of the Holy Spirit.

Many years ago, Charles Wesley, the brother of John and one of the greatest writers of hymns who has ever lived, wrote these words for Methodists to sing together: "Come, Holy Ghost, our hearts inspire, let us thy influence prove; / source of the old prophetic fire, fountain of life and love."[1] The language may be a bit out-of-date, but the message is not. As a people of faith, our first prayer together must be, "Come, Holy Spirit!" Why is this prayer so important? It is through the Holy Spirit that we are inspired and enabled to live as God would have us live. The Holy Spirit teaches us the ways of truth, inspires prophets, and is the source of continued life and love. Without the Holy Spirit, we can neither know the truth about God nor live in the ways in which God would have us live. In other words, God, through the Holy Spirit, teaches us and changes us.

In the very beginning of the Bible, the book of Genesis describes God's Spirit hovering over the waters (1:2).[2] The Spirit of God is present in the very first moments of creation, bringing order out of chaos. God's Spirit is associated with giving and sustaining life, as in Genesis 6:3. Continuing in this tradition, Psalm 104 cites God's Spirit as the source of creation and life. From this biblical perspective, life is a gift that the Spirit gives to us.

The Holy Spirit is present not simply at the beginning of creation, but also at the beginning of the Church. We call this event Pentecost, and we can read about it in Acts 2. Jesus tells his disciples in Acts 1:5, "You will be baptized with the Holy Spirit not many days from now," and in 1:8, "You will receive power when the Holy Spirit has come upon you." Then, while Jesus' followers and many other Jewish people are in Jerusalem for the Jewish festival of Pentecost,

> suddenly from heaven there came a sound like the rush of a violent wind, and it filled the entire house where they were sitting. Divided tongues, as of fire, appeared among them, and a tongue rested on each of them. All of them were filled with the Holy Spirit and began to speak in other languages, as the Spirit gave them ability (2:2-4).

Not only this, but also as the apostles spoke, the hearers who were present heard in their own languages. In Genesis 11:1-9, God confuses the languages of human beings because of their arrogance. Now, in service to the message about Jesus, God reverses this so that people can understand what Jesus' followers are saying. Even after the great miracles of Pentecost, the Holy Spirit continues to be present when people repent of their sins and are baptized (see 2:38; 8:15-17; 10:44-48; 19:6). The Holy Spirit might inspire people to praise God, speak in tongues, or prophesy. These ideas echo certain passages in the Old Testament, such as Joel 2:28: "Then afterward /

I will pour out my spirit on all flesh; / your sons and your daughters shall prophesy, / your old men shall dream dreams, / and your young men shall see visions."

The Gospel of John teaches us yet more about the Holy Spirit, and that the Spirit remains with us as a comforter, advocate, and teacher. Jesus has returned to the Father, but the Holy Spirit is alive and active among those who believe. Jesus calls the Spirit the Spirit of truth (14:17) who will continue to teach just as Jesus taught (14:26). Jesus even tells his disciples, "It is to your advantage that I go away, for if I do not go away, the Advocate [Holy Spirit] will not come to you; but if I go, I will send him to you" (16:7). The Holy Spirit, then, will lead Jesus' followers to understand his significance and message even more deeply than he led them to while he was among them. John is drawing upon a much older tradition, one we find in the Old Testament, in which the Spirit of God is seen as a teacher. For example, Nehemiah 9:20 speaks of the giving of God's Spirit to instruct Israel, and 9:30 speaks of the Spirit's warnings to Israel through the prophets. Likewise the psalmist prays, "Teach me to do your will, / for you are my God. / Let your good spirit lead me / on a level path" (Psalm 143:10). The Holy Spirit is a teacher—the most important teacher of all.

Yet knowing what to do is different from actually doing it. We can *know* what is right, but that does not mean that we will *do* what is right. In Romans, Paul puts the human condition this way: "I do not understand my own actions. For I do not do what I want, but I do the very thing I hate. . . . I can will what is right, but I cannot do it. For I do not do the good I want, but the evil I do not want is what I do" (Rom 7:15, 18-19). What, then, are we to do about this state of affairs? For Paul, the remedy comes when we become followers of Jesus, when we are baptized and join the community of people who know that Jesus is Lord. The Holy Spirit is alive and at work among this community of people (Rom 8:9). The Spirit brings Jesus Christ into our midst and gives us new life. "All who are led by the Spirit of God are children of God," says Paul (Rom 8:14). When we are adopted as God's children, we live life in the Spirit, and the Spirit empowers us to live as we know we should.

Within the so-called mainline traditions of Protestant Christianity we often neglect the work of the Holy Spirit. We tell people that we want them to go out and serve. We give them opportunities for mission. We often repeat the old heresy, "God has no hands but our hands," a statement that is neither accurate nor Christian, and is most certainly not Wesleyan. We extol the virtues of sacrificial giving and service, but we do not always provide the resources necessary for men and women to become the kind of people who will joyfully and continually engage in such work. Another way of putting this is to say that human beings are sinful (a topic discussed in chapter 5). Basically, this means that, left to our own devices, we will stray from God's will for our lives. We cannot overcome sinfulness on our own: we need God's help. By the power and work of the Holy Spirit, God creates within us a new heart, a new character. The Apostle Paul talks about an "old self" that we have before we are given over to Christ, a "self" that is replaced by new life in which we live as God would wish (see Rom 6:5-14). We can tell people again and again to do works of kindness, justice, love, and mercy, and they may indeed do these things, at least for a time. Christianity, however, is not about doing good deeds. It is about becoming a new kind of person, a person who lives as God wills, and this happens by the power and work of the Holy Spirit.

The Holy Spirit, then, is a teacher, a change agent, and an evangelist. The Holy Spirit is also a companion who comforts, sustains, and empowers. When people lose loved ones and we pray that God will comfort, strengthen, and sustain them in their loss, we are praying for the work of the Holy Spirit. When we pray for strength or wisdom to face a particular task, again we are praying for the work of the Spirit. By the Holy Spirit, God enables us to accomplish impossible tasks and endure great hardships.

The Holy Spirit has another important function as well: giving gifts to the Church. Paul writes in 1 Corinthians, "To each is given the manifestation of the Spirit for the common good. To one is given through the Spirit the utterance of wisdom, and to another the utterance of knowledge according to the same Spirit, to another faith by the same Spirit, to another gifts of healing by the one Spirit, to another the working of miracles, to another prophecy, to another the discernment of spirits, to another various kinds of tongues, to another the interpretation of tongues" (1 Cor 12:7-10). This is not an exhaustive list of the kinds of gifts the Spirit gives, but it shows the variety with which the Spirit gives gifts to the Church. Some Christian groups emphasize one particular gift over all the others. For example, some Pentecostal Christians believe that speaking in tongues, which is speaking in a divine language by the gift of the Holy Spirit, is necessary to demonstrate one's salvation. While Wesleyans may receive this gift, we do not see it as a necessary demonstration of salvation. With Paul, we believe that different people have different gifts, and that each of these gifts is useful for the building up of the Church. Some people may be gifted teachers, while others are healers, and still others are great preachers. Some people have the special gifts of bringing comfort to the sick, while others are gifted at working with children or youth. Regardless of the gift, we believe that their function is to build up the Church for doing God's will in the world.

A Lived Faith

The Wesleyan model for life is often described as a life of "holiness." This is a word that may mean different things to different people. In Wesleyan circles, however, it means living as God would have us live, something we can only consistently achieve by the power and work of the Holy Spirit. Remember what Paul said: we can know what is right, but this does not mean we are going to do it. Holiness, though, is about *both* knowing *and* doing. It is about right living in all of the different aspects of our lives. Fidelity in marriage, responsibility and generosity with our finances, conscientious parenting, proper care for our bodies, engaging consistently in works of love and kindness—all of these are part of the life to which God calls us, and that the Spirit enables us to live.

How does this happen, though? Does God simply choose who will receive the gifts of the Spirit that lead to lives of holiness? Some Christians believe that this is in fact what God does, but Wesleyans do not. We believe that the Holy Spirit is always calling to us, always reaching out to us, and it is our choice to say yes or no to the Spirit. Once we say yes to God, however, we also have the responsibility to *keep* saying yes to God. Wesleyans believe that, having once accepted the salvation that is ours in Christ, we can in fact ultimately reject that salvation and backslide into lives of sin. Therefore, after we say yes to God, there are some things that we should do. Wesley believed that prayer was an indispensible part of a healthy spiritual life. He was clear that every Christian should be a part of a church where he or she might continue to learn, grow, and be held accountable in the faith. He urged that Christians engage in the act of Holy Communion—the taking of the bread and the cup in Christian worship—as a way of keeping our relationship with God in good shape. (We will talk more about this in chapter 8.) He was deeply committed to consistent reading of the whole Bible because he believed that the Bible taught the way to salvation and that God worked through the Bible to lead us more deeply into the life of faith. He taught that our reading of Scripture should be closed with prayer, so that what we read "may be written on our hearts."[3]

These types of practices—prayer, worship, communion, reading Scripture—are what we sometimes call "spiritual disciplines." In other words, they are practices in which we should engage on a regular basis, even when we may not feel like it. Think about physical fitness for a moment. If we exercise every day and eat right, we will be healthier than if we lie around on the couch all of the time, eat chips, and drink soda. Further, if we only exercise when we feel especially motivated, we may *never* get off the couch. We have to have a certain amount of self-discipline to get in shape. Our spiritual lives are like that too, except it is not physical exercise and sustenance that we need, but spiritual. Worship, reading Scripture, communion, prayer, and other time-honored practices of Christians help us maintain healthy spiritual lives. We may not always feel like going to church or reading the Bible. We may not always be inspired to pray or yearn for the bread and cup of communion, but these practices are so deeply important to the life of faith that they must be practiced as disciplines.

Another way that we might talk about this is to say that the Christians who have gone before us in the faith have identified certain "means of grace." We can think of a "means of grace" as a special, spiritual connection between God and us. By the means of grace, we receive the Holy Spirit, and the Spirit thus helps us become the people God wants us to be. We will at times still be tempted to live selfishly, to act in ways that we know are wrong, but by the power and work of the Holy Spirit, we not only know what is right, we also now have the power to do it. From a Wesleyan perspective, that is the main way in which the Spirit affects our everyday lives. Yes, the Holy Spirit does work miracles such as healing the sick and inspiring words of prophecy and tongues, but these are extraordinary gifts of the Spirit. In the everyday grind of life, we may not often see things that we would so clearly identify as miracles. But if we are attentive to the means of grace, we can feel the Spirit's work in changing our wills to be more like the will of God.

A Deeper Faith

The twentieth century has witnessed an explosion of interest in the work of the Holy Spirit. In part this has stemmed from developments within the Wesleyan tradition. After coming to terms with the doctrine of the inner witness of the Holy Spirit in the human heart and the secret working of the Holy Spirit in the means of grace, folk began asking questions about the miraculous action of the Holy Spirit in healing, contemporary prophecy, and speaking in tongues. This interest blossomed within the Holiness Movement of the nineteenth century, in which there developed a fascination with the early chapters of the book of Acts. In Acts 2 there is clearly a profound encounter with the Holy Spirit that in turn involves all sorts of interesting miraculous activity. In time the Pentecostal tradition goes all out to recover the miraculous, takes off on a life of its own, and spreads across the world. Ironically, the Holiness Movement initially rejected the child it brought to birth in Pentecostalism. This life-affirming and miraculous version of Christianity cycles back in the charismatic movement within mainline Protestant and Catholic Christianity. In a revised form it shows up in the most vibrant form of Christianity, which has spread like wildfire in developing nations outside of Europe and North America. It is now beginning to get the attention and examination it deserves.

The crucial issue is what to make of the more sensational gifts of the Spirit, like healing and speaking in tongues. Are these genuine? Were they real in the early days of the Church but are no longer needed today? If they are genuine, how should we understand them? And how might they be brought into the life and ministry of the Church without causing chaos or splits? Just as it took a lot of time for Wesley to sort out what happened to him when he experienced the Holy Spirit at Aldersgate, it will also take years for the Church to work through what to do with the gifts of the Holy Spirit.

Certain things are already clear. First, these gifts never really died out in the history of the Church; they were buried beneath the surface and kept alive in the margins; so they should be welcomed by Christians today. Second, the gifts should never be separated from the fruit of the Spirit manifest in love, joy, peace, patience, kindness, goodness, faithfulness, gentleness, and self-control (Gal 5:22). Third, the gifts are given sovereignly by God; they are not given at our demand or because we want them. The Holy Spirit is in charge; we are not. Fourth, all the gifts are given for the common good; they are not given so that we can boast or make a fuss about them in an effort to bolster our pride. If we misuse them, we will simply wreck our own spiritual lives and the inner harmony of the Church.

In thinking about the gifts of the Spirit, some Christians turn against the institutional life of the Church, railing against the power plays and bureaucracy that so often suffocate the life of the Church. So they go off on their own to practice the gifts in small groups or renewal movements. This is a serious mistake. The Holy Spirit gives gifts to individuals not only for their ministry but also for creating the Church and giving spiritual offices to secure the welfare of the Church across space and time. Hence the Holy Spirit calls and equips individuals to become deacons, elders, and bishops who safeguard the life of the Church across the generations. These offices are wonderful gifts of the Spirit. So the solution to this problem is to expand our understanding of how the Spirit works rather than to cut back on the gifts of the Spirit. Clearly we have a lot of thinking, praying, and practicing to do up ahead if we are to come to terms with the fullness of the work of the Holy Spirit in the Church today.

The Catechism

God the Holy Spirit

Q. Who is God the Holy Spirit?

A. The Third Person of the Trinity, who proceeds from the Father and the Son.[4]

> "When the Advocate comes, whom I will send to you from the Father, the Spirit of truth who comes from the Father, he will testify on my behalf" (John 15:26).

> "These things God has revealed to us through the Spirit; for the Spirit searches everything, even the depths of God" (1 Cor 2:10).

Q. How does God relate to us through the Holy Spirit?

A. The Holy Spirit convinces human beings of sin, righteousness, and judgment; leads us into faithful response to the gospel; comforts, sustains, and empowers the righteous; and leads us into all truth.[5]

> "Therefore I want you to understand that no one speaking by the Spirit of God ever says 'Let Jesus be cursed!' and no one can say 'Jesus is Lord' except by the Holy Spirit" (1 Cor 12:3).

Q. How can we come to know Jesus Christ?

A. We come to know Jesus Christ because the Holy Spirit mediates Christ to us.

Q. How can we receive the Holy Spirit?

A. Through means of grace, such as the sacraments, prayer, worship, and reading Scripture.

Q. What will be the effect of the Spirit's work in my life?

A. Renewed life in the present and eternal life with God.

> "Jesus answered, 'Very truly, I tell you, no one can enter the kingdom of God without being born of water and Spirit. What is born of the flesh is flesh, and what is born of the Spirit is spirit'" (John 3:5-6).

> "So if anyone is in Christ, there is a new creation: everything old has passed away; see, everything has become new!" (2 Cor 5:17).

> "He saved us, not because of any works of righteousness that we had done, but according to his mercy, through the water of rebirth and renewal by the Holy Spirit. This Spirit he poured out on us richly through Jesus Christ our Savior" (Titus 3:5-6).

Q. How do we recognize the presence of the Holy Spirit in our lives?[6]

A. We recognize the presence of the Holy Spirit when we confess Jesus Christ as Lord and are made partakers of the divine nature.

"And this is what some of you used to be. But you were washed, you were sanctified, you were justified in the name of the Lord Jesus Christ and in the Spirit of our God" (1 Cor 6:11).

Q. How can we recognize the truths taught by the Holy Spirit?[7]

A. We recognize them when they accord with the Scriptures, are consistent with the traditions of the Church, and by their moral and ethical coherence with Christian faith and practice.[8]

"I will put my spirit within you, and make you follow my statutes and be careful to observe my ordinances" (Ezek 36:27).

"When the Spirit of truth comes, he will guide you into all the truth; for he will not speak on his own, but will speak whatever he hears, and he will declare to you the things that are to come" (John 16:13).

"Those who are unspiritual do not receive the gifts of God's Spirit, for they are foolishness to them, and they are unable to understand them because they are spiritually discerned" (1 Cor 2:14).

Q. Can we resist the work of the Spirit?

A. Yes, but in so doing we put our salvation at risk.

"Do not be deceived; God is not mocked, for you reap whatever you sow. If you sow to your own flesh, you will reap corruption from the flesh; but if you sow to the Spirit, you will reap eternal life from the Spirit" (Gal 6:7-8).

In Your Own Words

1. The Holy Spirit is the abiding presence of God in our lives that teaches and changes us so that we become more like Jesus. Looking at your own spiritual journey, where are you? At the beginning? About halfway? Moving toward the finish line? What have you learned? How are you different today than when you first started?

2. The Holy Spirit teaches us the ways of truth, inspires prophets, and is the source of continued life and love within individuals, but also in the Church, God's community. How does your church reflect the presence of God? How open is your group or church to the promptings of the Holy Spirit? How do you test or discern the Spirit to see if the promptings are truly from God?

3. Do you have plans that can only happen with the help of the Holy Spirit? Does your church? If all things were possible, how would you plan differently? What is your church doing that will only happen if the Holy Spirit works on your behalf?

4. Is there a place in your life where you need to say yes to God? How does it help you to surround yourself with other faithful believers?

5. Share your thoughts about what it means to live a grace-filled life. How might it involve practicing the spiritual disciplines? How does your church introduce people to the spiritual disciplines? Which do you find most helpful? Most difficult?

6. Do you believe in miracles? Has a miracle ever happened to you or someone you know?

7. What are the gifts of the Holy Spirit and how do you understand them? Which have you experienced? Which are needed in your church today?

4 What Are Human Beings?

A Wesleyan Faith

John Wesley's first university sermon, preached in the church at Oxford University in 1730, is titled "The Image of God."[1] It is a sermon that discusses what it means to think about human nature from a specifically Christian perspective. Much of this sermon has to do with the issue of human sin, but from the very beginning Wesley asserts one crucial point: human beings are created in the image of God. In light of the fact that all people share this characteristic as part of their nature, he finds it odd that this truth is not universally acknowledged. Quite objectionable, he says, is the idea that we are more like beasts than like God.

The idea that human beings are created in the image of God has its origin in the first chapter of the Bible. We read in Genesis 1:26-27:

> Then God said, "Let us make humankind in our image, according to our likeness; and let them have dominion over the fish of the sea, and over the birds of the air, and over the cattle, and over all the wild animals of the earth, and over every creeping thing that creeps upon the earth."

> So God created humankind in his image,
>> in the image of God he created them,
>> male and female he created them.

Sometimes people are curious about why the text says, "Let *us* make humankind in *our* image." Why "us" and "our" rather than "me" and "my"? In this passage, God is presented as a divine king surrounded by a court of other divine beings. Think of God surrounded by angels, speaking to them about the creation of human beings. The humans are not going to be created in the image of beasts, but in the divine image. Humans are not simply one more species of the animal kingdom. Rather, they have authority over the animals, over all the earth, in fact. Humans represent a different kind of creation than all that has been created before. Like God, we have will, reason, and morality.

Psalm 8 expresses basically the same idea, affirming that God has made human beings "a little lower than God, / and crowned them with glory and honor" (Ps 8:5). The Hebrew word that the NRSV translates as "God" in this passage is *elohim*, and it could be translated in a number of ways. In fact, the NIV translates this passage, "You have made [human beings] a little lower than the angels." Nevertheless, the point is clear: human beings hold a very special place within creation.

It is, in fact, as one of these beings who are "a little lower" than those who dwell in heaven, that God came to us in Jesus Christ. This is exactly how the writer of the Letter to the Hebrews reads Psalm 8 as a prophecy about Jesus. This writer (and we do not know who wrote it) holds that Jesus, who became "a little lower than the angels," is now "crowned with glory and honor because of the suffering of death" (Heb 2:9). In other words, having become human, Jesus died for all people, and for that reason is honored more highly than any other of the divine beings.

The problem with the claim that human beings are created in the image of God is that we often act so contrary to God's will. In other words, human beings sin. Wesley understood that those who disagreed with his understanding of human beings would emphasize our wrongdoing: "A fine picture—this ignorant, wretched, guilty creature—of a wise, happy, and holy Creator!"[2] He did of course recognize that humans sin, but this did not undercut for him the notion that we are *created* in the divine image. Rather, he believed, that through sin we actually *lose* the image of God. Traits such as understanding, the desire and freedom to act in keeping with God's wishes, a loving disposition, and happiness—these are all traits of the divine image. Nevertheless, when we look at the world, again and again we see people *not* exemplifying these kinds of traits. Therefore, even though we are created in the image of God, we lose that image through sin.

The Bible teaches again and again that, while human beings are created in the divine image, we do not always live like it. The story of Adam, Eve, and the forbidden fruit in the Garden of Eden (Gen 3) is a story about how humans defied God. In fact, they tried to be *like* God. The serpent enticed Eve into disobeying God by telling her that when she eats the forbidden fruit, "your eyes will be opened, and you will be like God, knowing good and evil" (Gen 3:5). Adam apparently needs no such enticement. He simply eats what is given to him. Then we read that the snake was in fact right: once Adam and Eve ate of the fruit, "the eyes of both were opened" (3:7). They were created in the image of God, but that was not enough. They wanted to be *more* like God, and they reached too far. This sin has repeated itself again and again through history: humans confuse their role with God's role, and the results are catastrophic.

This, of course, is not the end of the story. Through Jesus Christ, we have the ability to recover the image of God. Greater understanding, a will that is like God's will, love toward others, and true happiness are ours through Jesus Christ. These are ours after what Wesley called "new birth," a topic that we will learn more about in chapter 6. But for now it suffices to say that when our will is at odds with God's will, when we seek to go our own way instead of God's way, we who are *created* in God's image fail to *reflect* that image. Wesley believed that human sin causes us to be like untuned instruments: "The instrument being now quite untuned, she could no longer make the same harmony."[3] We are no longer in harmony with God's will.

Not everyone who hears the message about Jesus Christ will accept it and return to God, from whom they are estranged. People, after all, have free will when it comes to doing good or evil. It is important to realize that not all Christians believe that human beings have free will. Some believe that human beings are so corrupt through sin that we cannot even recognize our own sinfulness, and we are therefore incapable of turning back to God. How is it that some people accept Christ, then? God overrides their sinful nature through a powerful and irresistible act of divine grace (a word that in this context refers to a gift that we have not earned), and once they realize their sin and God's goodness, their lives are never the same. These people never give up their salvation; such is the nature of God's powerful work on the human will. Wesleyans, however, have a different perspective. We believe that God's Holy Spirit is at work on all people all of the time, enabling anyone who wishes to accept God's gift of salvation to do so. Nevertheless, we do not *have to* do so. We can in fact say no to God. God's grace is not irresistible. Further, once we've said yes to God, we can still, at a later time, turn around and say "no." We human beings have free will, and God does not force our hand to make us do what is right for us and best for the world.

It is important to realize, though, that when human beings defy God and act in ways that are contrary to God's will, these kinds of actions do not nullify God's love for us nor the importance of human life. In fact, one of the most basic truths of Christian faith is that God loves us *while we are sinners*, and the salvation that God offers us is a proof of that love. The apostle Paul states this explicitly in his Letter to the Romans: "God proves his love for us in that while we still were sinners Christ died for us" (Rom 5:8). Human beings matter. Whether Christian or non-Christian, righteous, sinful, or somewhere in between, human beings matter. We matter so much, in fact, that the Son of God died on a cross for us. Paul says in the same letter, "For I am convinced that neither death, nor life, nor angels, nor rulers, nor things present, nor things to come, nor powers, nor height, nor depth, nor anything else in all creation, will be able to separate us from the love of God in Christ Jesus our Lord" (Rom 8:38).

A Lived Faith

What does it mean to take seriously the fact that we are created by God in the image of God? What does it mean that God loves us enough, even in the midst of our sin, to come to us in Jesus Christ and die for us upon the cross? Sometimes Christianity is presented as a list of "don'ts": don't smoke, don't drink, don't have extramarital sex, and so on. These "don'ts," however, are really only the negative side of saying something much more positive: *Do* live like you are a being of sacred worth, and like other people are too. When we use tobacco we hurt our bodies and endanger our lives, which are gifts to us from God. Too much alcohol can lead to out-of-control behavior, addiction, abuse of other people, and even death. When we engage in illicit or casual sexual behavior, we degrade ourselves, acting as if our bodies were mere instruments of pleasure, rather than gifts from God that allow us to live in and interact with God's good creation.

The same could be said for our habits around diet and exercise. While in some Christian traditions gluttony is often mentioned as a sin, in many traditions it goes unmentioned. Nevertheless, if we are of sacred worth as human beings, if we are created in the image of God, then what we put into our bodies and how we take care of our bodies really does matter. Imagine that each week when you went to church, the altar at the front leaned to one side, the chairs or pews were stained and needed a thorough cleaning, and half of the light bulbs had burned out. Imagine that there were stains on the floor and walls, and broken windows. A newcomer to the church would likely ask, "*Who's taking care of this place?*" The answer, of course, would be that nobody is taking care of it. Despite that it is a sacred place where people come together to worship God, no one is caring for it and therefore it has fallen into disrepair. Good things may continue to happen there, of course, but the ways in which the congregants have cared for the building does say something about the value that they assign to their place of worship. In the same way, our bodies are sacred places. We did not build them. Rather, God gave them to us, and like a church building, they are given to us to honor and serve God. If we are properly to honor God, then, we should take care of the bodies that God has given to us. This is no less the case for people with disabilities than the able-bodied. The value of a human being comes from his or her God-given nature, rather than from some notion of functionality. So whether able-bodied or disabled, we matter, our bodies matter, and we should care for ourselves as people of sacred worth.

Self-care, however, is only a part of what's at stake in realizing the value of human beings. Being a Christian is not just about the care of the self, or even only about loving God, but the care of others. As we read in 1 John 4:21, "those who love God must love their brothers and sisters also." Again, human beings really do matter. They matter enough for Christ to die for us. If this is the case, this must affect the way in which we live each and every day, and this can complicate life considerably and raise a host of questions for us. For example, how are we going to treat the person in the office whom no one likes? How are we going to regard those people with whom we disagree politically? How does our understanding of human beings come to bear, for example, on issues such as illegal immigration? Under what circumstances, if any, is it permissible for Christians to use violence against other people? How should we react to issues of poverty, both locally and globally? Do we treat our spouses and children as created in the image of God, as creatures of sacred worth? Some of these questions are easier to answer than others, but in answering any of them we need to keep in mind what we say about human beings not simply from scientific, political, or economic perspectives, but from a specifically *Christian* perspective.

We could discuss many other examples of how Wesleyans should or should not live. We could create another list of "don'ts." The important thing, however, is not some list of particular things we should and should not do, but the basic principle involved: our lives as human beings really do matter. How we treat ourselves and other people really does matter. Human beings are creatures of sacred worth, and if we believe this, then we need to live like it.

A Deeper Faith

It is crucial for Christians to keep in mind that a person's humanity is determined entirely by his or her being created by God in the image of God. Nevertheless, we commonly see people dehumanized for a variety of reasons. For example, it is commonplace in times of war for people to dehumanize their enemies, casting them within a kind of group identity and labeling them with terms such as *infidels, commies,* or other such terms, some of which are actually much more degrading than these. To regard other people in this way—to assign them an identity that categorizes them within a larger group but does not account for their individual humanity—is profoundly unchristian.

Wesley faced a huge crisis of dehumanization in his day: the crisis of slavery. When he addressed this crisis, he did so in part by emphasizing the common human characteristics of these captive people. He castigates the slavers, saying,

> You have seen them torn away,—children from their parents, parents from their children; husbands from their wives, wives from their beloved husbands, brethren and sisters from each other. You have dragged them who had never done you any wrong, perhaps in chains, from their native shore. You have forced them into your ships like an herd of swine,—them who had souls immortal as your own.[4]

He asks, "Did the Creator intend that the noblest creatures in the visible world should live such a life as this?"[5] Wesley would not accept the dehumanization of slaves by those who would exploit them for economic advantage.

Today we face complex ethical debates around such issues as severe disability, healthcare, abortion, and end-of-life care. These issues are difficult, and there is not room here to offer them the considered attention that such serious matters deserve. Nevertheless, what we must not allow is the equating of humanity with functionality. In other words, we are human because God has created us as human, not because of what we are able to do, think, or say. If we are confined to bed, or even apparently unable to respond to stimuli (which we often designate with the dehumanizing term *vegetative state*), we are still human. For that reason, all people, whether born or unborn, entirely able-bodied or disabled, responsive or unresponsive, young or old, are equally human. Our humanity is not dependent on what we can *do*. Like our salvation, it is a gift from God.

The Catechism

Human Beings

Q. What are we by nature?

A. We are part of God's creation, made in the image of God.[6]

> "Then God said, 'Let us make humankind in our image, according to our likeness; and let them have dominion over the fish of the sea, and over the birds of the air, and over the cattle, and over all the wild animals of the earth, and over every creeping thing that creeps upon the earth.'
> So God created humankind in his image,
> in the image of God he created them;
> male and female he created them" (Gen 1:26-27).

> "Then the LORD God formed man from the dust of the ground, and breathed into his nostrils the breath of life; and the man became a living being" (Gen 2:7).

> "But from the beginning of creation, 'God made them male and female'" (Mark 10:6).

Q. What does it mean to be created in the image of God?

A. It means that we are free to make choices: to love, to create, to reason, and to live in harmony with creation and with God.[7]

Q. Why then do we live apart from God and out of harmony with creation?

A. Human beings have free will, and from the beginning we have misused our freedom and made wrong choices.[8]

> "Now the serpent was more crafty than any other wild animal that the Lord God had made. He said to the woman, 'Did God say, "You shall not eat from any tree in the garden"?' The woman said to the serpent, 'We may eat of the fruit of the trees in the garden; but God said, "You shall not eat of the fruit of the tree that is in the middle of the garden, nor shall you touch it, or you shall die."' But the serpent said to the woman, 'You will not die; for God knows that when you eat of it your eyes will be opened, and you will be like God, knowing good and evil.' So when the woman saw that the tree was good for food, and that it was a delight to the eyes, and that the tree was to be desired to make one wise, she took of its fruit and ate; and she also gave some to her husband, who was with her, and he ate. Then the eyes of both were opened, and they knew that they were naked; and they sewed fig leaves together and made loincloths for themselves" (Gen 3:1-7).

Q. What is this misuse of our freedom and making of wrong choices called?

A. It is called sin.

> "For out of the heart come evil intentions, murder, adultery, fornication, theft, false witness, slander" (Matt 15:19).

> "For the wages of sin is death, but the free gift of God is eternal life in Christ Jesus our Lord" (Rom 6:23).

"For I know that nothing good dwells within me, that is, in my flesh. I can will what is right, but I cannot do it. For I do not do the good I want, but the evil I do not want is what I do" (Rom 7:18-19).

"For this reason the mind that is set on the flesh is hostile to God; it does not submit to God's law—indeed it cannot" (Rom 8:7).

Q. Why do we not use our freedom as we should?

A. Apart from the grace of our Lord Jesus Christ, humankind is destitute of holiness and inclined to evil.[9]

Q. What help is there for us?

A. Our help is in God.[10]

"No one can see the kingdom of God without being born from above" (John 3:3).

Q. How has God helped us?

A. By acting in history through prophets, seers, and saints; by Jesus Christ, who reconciles us to the Father; and by the Holy Spirit, who abides with us and helps us to know the Son and the Father.

In Your Own Words

1. We are created in the image of God. Share how seeing others as created in God's image might make you see them differently. How can you cultivate seeing the image of God in other people, your family, your friends, your rivals, your enemies?

2. We all make mistakes; we all tend to confuse our role with God's; we all sin and fall short of the glory of God. How can we stop confusing our role with God's role? What is our role in relation to God?

3. What is God's will for us as humans? For you as a person? Do you believe that God is happy with your current choices?

4. As God's children, we are free to reflect God's image and we are free to choose to reflect something else. What does your life reflect? What values? What goals? What achievements?

5. How well do you take care of your body, your soul, your significant relationships, your church? How much time do you devote to each? How can God help you take care of the things you need to do? How can God help you prioritize?

6. How might understanding all human beings as being created in the image of God change the debates about disability, and beginning-of-life and end-of-life care?

5 What Is Sin?

A Wesleyan Faith

Wesley was irked by people who thought too well of themselves, or thought too highly of human nature in general. Indeed, Wesley did believe that all people are created in the image of God, but he certainly did not believe that people were generally, in their present state, "innocent and wise and virtuous."[1] He scoffed at the idea that a person has "all virtue and happiness in his composition, or at least entirely in his power, without being beholden to any other being."[2] There were of course champions of this kind of position in Wesley's day, just as there are today. Nevertheless, in response to this view of human nature he asks, "What must we do with our Bibles? For they will never agree with this."[3] In other words, a Wesleyan view of human beings must reckon with the fact that all people sin.

What is sin? It is the violation of God's will. Often we hear talk of "original sin." Wesley certainly believed in the power of original sin. The topic comes up frequently in his sermons. Basically, original sin is the idea that human beings cannot help but think, act, and speak in ways that violate God's will—until, that is, God goes to work on them, changing them from the inside out. This is an old idea with its roots in the writings of the Apostle Paul. If Paul provided the raw material for it, however, the fourth- and fifth-century Christian thinker Augustine of Hippo sent it into mass production.

Augustine, taking his cues from Paul (see Rom 5:12-21), goes all the way back to the story of Adam and Eve in the book of Genesis. He says that when Adam and Eve disobeyed God and ate the fruit of the tree of knowledge of good and evil, fruit that was forbidden to them, they committed the very first sin, the "original" sin (see Genesis 3). The perfect and sinless state in which they had lived was therefore corrupted. Both sin and death came into the world through this act. Furthermore, all human beings after Adam and Eve inherited two unfortunate legacies. First, because the perfection of humankind was broken, all human beings thereafter have no choice but to sin, unless they are saved through Jesus Christ. In our normal state, we no longer desire God. Rather, we love and desire everything but God, as if these other things *were* God. Second, all human beings inherit the guilt of sin through Adam and Eve. They are born with that guilt, and it must be removed through baptism and faith in Jesus Christ.

This account of sin has done a lot of heavy lifting over the years. Many, many Christians have found it compelling. Whether or not we find Augustine's account of the origins of sin satisfactory, we can approach the idea of original sin this way: if we look around at the world, we see violations of God's will everywhere. On a small scale, we might see this in gossip at work, in kids becoming targets of bullies on the playground, in lies between husbands and wives, in petty theft, or in sexual promiscuity. On a grand scale, we see such problems as global poverty, genocide, and racial hatred. There are, moreover, both sins of *commission* and sins of *omission*. When we actively engage in sinful behavior or social structures, our sin is one of commission. But simply standing by while injustice happens, doing nothing in the face of evil when we have the capacity to challenge it, is a sin of omission. We may not have done anything wrong, but we failed to do anything right. As we read in James 4:17, "Anyone . . . who knows the right thing to do and fails to do it, commits sin." Sin is all around us all the time. Regardless of how things got this way, the problem remains that sin runs deep, is pervasive in this world, and has serious consequences.

Sometimes the Apostle Paul talks about sin the way in which some Christians talk about the devil, or Satan. Sin, for Paul, is a cosmic force that acts upon human beings, pushing them into wrong choices, keeping them from being in right relationship with God. Paul says that all people are "under the power of sin" (Rom 3:9), and when he sins, "it is no longer I that do it, but sin that dwells within me" (Rom 7:17). Sin is not simply something that people do—it has a *spiritual* component as well. Many Christians have believed that, just as God gave free will to humans, God gave free will to angels, and that some of them turned against God. The chief among these is known as Satan, a name that comes from the Hebrew word for *accuser* or *adversary*. Sometimes in the Bible, Satan acts like God's district attorney, attempting to show the guilt, or at least the evil tendencies, of human beings (see Job 1:6-12; Zech 3:1). At other times, Satan is characterized as a tempter who opposes God's purposes. We even see Satan trying to tempt Jesus at times (Matt 4:1-11; Mark 1:12-13; Luke 4:1-13). In 1 Peter, Satan is characterized as a prowling, roaring lion that wishes to devour human beings (1 Pet 5:8). John Wesley certainly believed in demons and the effects that they had on people. While this kind of belief has diminished considerably in the United States and Western Europe, most Christians worldwide believe strongly in evil spiritual forces. It is also worth noting that within the ritual of baptism in The United Methodist Church, people are still asked if they denounce the spiritual forces of wickedness.

A Lived Faith

It is helpful for us as people of faith to be aware of the human propensity to sin. The Letter of James talks about the ways in which we might find ourselves struggling with conflicting desires. On the one hand, we may know the right thing to do. We may wish to do the right thing as well. At the same time, however, we may wish to do something that we should not, something that is at cross purposes with God's will. James calls this being "double-minded" (1:8). This term refers to competing impulses within us, rather like Paul discusses in Romans 7:15 when he says, "I do not understand my own actions. For I do not do what I want, but I do the very thing I hate." Christians have long talked about the temptation to sin, the desire that is in us to think, act, and speak in ways that God does not will for us. James talks about it in this way: "One is tempted by one's own desire, being lured and enticed by it; then, when that desire has conceived, it gives birth to sin, and that sin, when it is fully grown, gives birth to death" (1:14-15). It is simply a part of the human condition that at times we *will* want to think, speak, and do things that God does not wish. We should expect this to happen, and when it does, God allows us to choose the right way or the wrong way to live. When we choose the wrong way, however, we should not expect to find lasting happiness. Only in God can we find lasting happiness and true fulfillment.

We do well to recognize that we, as people, are not complete on our own, and that we need God to help us live well and find true happiness. In his famous book, *Confessions*, Augustine writes in prayer to God, "you have made us for yourself, and our heart is restless until it rests in you."[4] Only in God can we truly find fulfillment, and when we try to find it in other things, such as money, clothing, sex, food, alcohol, drugs, shopping, sports, or any other of the many, many things we use to distract ourselves, we will fail. We are setting up idols where God should be. This way of doing things is bound to lead to a continued sense of emptiness and sorrow, and the more we continue on this path, the more likely we are to commit sin after sin, never properly honoring God as we should.

Think about the sensation of buying a new car, of driving it for the first time. It has that new-car smell. The engine runs perfectly (one hopes). The wheels are balanced, the sound system is clear, and the wipers leave not a droplet of moisture behind them. You look forward to driving it—for a while. But eventually, the new-car smell goes away, a coffee stain may appear here or there, the engine may knock, the sound system may stop working. Any number of things may happen. More significant than any of this, however, the car simply becomes part of your routine, part of the everyday fabric of your life. When you get in your car to drive to work every day for a year, two years, or longer, you probably will not even think much about the car itself. Inevitably, you will eventually want a new car, which will in time be replaced by yet another new car. The same could be said about a favorite restaurant, a new television, or a new outfit. No matter how much we pay for them, how hard we work to get them, or how nice they look in the store, the pleasure of such things fades away. Jesus warned us about this, saying, "one's life does not consist in the abundance of one's possessions" (Luke 12:15).

The prophet Isaiah writes, "The grass withers, the flower fades; but the word of our God will stand forever" (40:8). Only God can give us true happiness. Yes, things can give us pleasure, and there is nothing wrong with this, but things cannot bring us lasting and true happiness. Everything in our lives—our cars, our homes, our money, our clothes, are God's, and should be used in ways that serve God. The same could be said for people. Superficial and shallow relationships cannot bring us happiness. But a friendship, marriage, or other meaningful relationship that is rooted in the love of God and in a desire to serve God can bring great happiness and fulfillment. As Christians, we believe God is the source of all good gifts. God is the source of all true happiness. All that we own belongs to God. Our relationships belong to God. Therefore, we must be mindful at all times that our lives, and everything in them, are God's. God loves us, and we belong to God. When we begin to use the things or people in our lives selfishly, we are misusing the freedom that God has given us, and we commit sin. As Augustine put it, "The good things which you love are all from God, but they are good and sweet only as long as they are used to do his will. They will rightly turn bitter if God is spurned and the things that come from him are wrongly loved."[5]

A Deeper Faith

In Mark 2:27, Jesus says, "The sabbath was made for humankind, and not humankind for the sabbath." This saying might sound a bit odd to us today, but it has far-reaching implications. The sabbath is a day set aside for rest and for honor of God. In Judaism there are strict rules around sabbath observance. In fact, this is stipulated within the Ten Commandments: "Observe the sabbath day and keep it holy" (Deut 5:12). Jesus, however, is saying that God did not make people simply to follow rules. Rather, the rules are there for the benefit of people. God's way of doing things leads us into ways of life, rather than ways of death. God's way of doing things leads us to flourish as people.

It seems sometimes that among Christians the rules become their own end. Our faith becomes rule-centered, rather than grace-centered. Rules are certainly important, but they are important because they lead us into a proper relationship with God. Take a commonplace example like smoking. Christians are right to say that smoking is not consistent with the Christian life, but why? Because cigarette smoke offends God? Of course not. Rather, the reason is that God wishes us to care for our bodies and to use our bodies in ways that honor the fact that they are gifts from God. Smoking, however, hurts our bodies. It can even kill us. God's will is for our well-being, so habits that diminish our well-being are not in keeping with God's will. We humans are not made simply to obey rules.

Rather, God leads us to establish particular rules and guidelines for living within our communities so that we can flourish as God wishes.

The Catechism

Sin

Q. What is sin?

A. Sin is the violation of God's will.

Q. By whom was sin brought into the world?

A. Sin was brought into the world by Satan, and by human beings who have yielded to Satan's temptations.[6]

Q. Who is Satan?

A. Satan was once a holy angel, but fell away from God.[7]

> "God did not spare the angels when they sinned, but cast them into hell and committed them to chains of deepest darkness to be kept until the judgment" (2 Pet 2:4).

Q. Do all people sin?

A. Yes, all people have sinned and fall short of the glory of God (Rom 3:23).

Q. What is original sin?

A. Original sin is the corruption of the image of God within human beings.

"Indeed, I was born guilty,
a sinner when my mother conceived me" (Ps 51:5).

Q. What is the result of original sin?

A. We do not truly love and serve God as we should, and we cannot help but commit actual sin.

"For I know that nothing good dwells within me, that is, in my flesh. I can will what is right, but I cannot do it. For I do not do the good I want, but the evil I do not want is what I do" (Rom 7:18-19).

Q. What is actual sin?

A. Actual sin is every thought, word, and deed by which we violate God's will.

Q. What is personal sin?

A. Personal sin is an actual sin that results from an individual's thought, word, or deed.

Q. What is social sin?

A. Social sin is the participation in sinful social structures.

Q. Where is our salvation from sin?

A. Our salvation from sin is in Jesus Christ.

"The next day he saw Jesus coming toward him and declared, 'Here is the Lamb of God who takes away the sin of the world!'" (John 1:29).

"In him we have redemption through his blood, the forgiveness of our trespasses, according to the riches of his grace" (Eph 1:7).

"He is the atoning sacrifice for our sins, and not for ours only but also for the sins of the whole world" (1 John 2:2).

In Your Own Words

1. For many, original sin is a difficult idea to grasp. How do you understand sin? Is there a difference between sins and original sin? What are the consequences of believing and not believing in sin?

2. Give some examples of the sins of commission and the sins of omission.

3. We are all tempted. What are some strategies to beat temptation?

4. Some people say, "the devil made me do it." What do you believe about Satan, evil, and the spiritual forces of wickedness?

5. What kinds of rules and guidelines are helpful (or are they?) in helping people overcome sin and temptation? What kinds of guidelines does your church have in place to help prevent fraud, sexual abuse, theft, and so forth? What happens if one of the church leaders or members falls?

6 What Is Salvation?

A Wesleyan Faith

In 1782, Wesley wrote that some years before, four factories for spinning and weaving had been set up in the town of Epworth. Employed within these factories were many young men and women, even boys and girls. As Wesley describes their manner, "The whole conversation of these was profane and loose to the last degree." Wesley notes, however, that a few of these workers stumbled into one of his prayer meetings and "were suddenly cut to the heart." They immediately went out to gather their companions and bring them to the prayer meeting. After this,

> The whole scene was changed. In three of the factories, no more lewdness or profaneness was found, for God had put a new song in their mouth, and blasphemies were turned to praise. Those three I visited today, and I found religion had taken deep root in them. No trifling word was heard among them, and they watch over each other in love. I found it exceedingly good to be there, and we rejoiced together in the God of our salvation.[1]

From a Wesleyan perspective, we would say that these young people were being saved. The terms *saved* and *salvation* sometimes bring with them no small amount of baggage in Christian circles, so it will be important for us to understand what Wesleyans mean when we use them. Sometimes among Christians the term *salvation* means basically that one is saved from God's wrath. The idea goes like this: God cannot be in the presence of sin, and all human beings are guilty of sin. The price of sin is eternal punishment, but God, by becoming human in Jesus Christ and dying on the cross, has paid the necessary price for our sin. By putting our faith in Jesus Christ, we can receive the salvation that God has worked out for us on the cross. In essence, then, salvation means that one has secured a place eternally with God and avoided the punishment of sinners in hell.

A Wesleyan understanding of salvation, however, is far more complex than this, and far richer as well. Eternal life with God is clearly part of salvation, but that is the *final stage* of salvation, which is called *glorification.* Wesley's sermon "The Scripture Way of Salvation," which is possibly his most influential, is of great help to us in understanding the ways in which he thought about salvation. He says in this sermon that salvation is not simply "the soul's going to paradise," not simply "a blessing which lies on the other side of death." He goes on, "It is not something at a distance: it is a present thing, a blessing which, through the free mercy of God, ye are now in possession of." In essence, salvation, for Wesley, is "the entire work of God," from the first stirring in our souls telling us that we need God to our receiving of eternal life.[2]

Sometimes Wesleyans talk about salvation in terms of various demonstrations of God's grace. When Christians use the word *grace*, it simply means a gift from God. It is not something that we earn, but something that God gives to us out of love. Among Wesleyans, we often use it to talk about the work of the Holy Spirit in our lives. For example, Wesley talks in "The Scripture Way of Salvation" about what he terms *preventing* grace, also sometimes called *prevenient* grace. Here the term *preventing* does not mean "stopping," but rather it has an older meaning of "going before." Before we ever reach out to God, God reaches out to us. The Holy Spirit draws us to God, calling us into a loving, life-giving relationship with God, and creating within us a desire to know and love God. Unfortunately, says Wesley, people very often stifle these desires, and soon forget that they were ever there.[3] God does not force us into belief or faith. We have a choice to accept or reject the Holy Spirit's work in our lives.

Saying yes to the work of the Spirit means that we repent of our old way of living and accept God's new ways of living. The word *repent* means not just feeling sorry for what we have done, but orienting our lives toward God's purposes. In the Gospel of Luke, Jesus meets a man named Zacchaeus who is a tax collector. Tax collectors were widely disliked for a few reasons, but one is that they were considered dishonest. They could make profit by collecting more than was required, thus putting an additional financial burden on people who had very little. Whereas many people shunned tax collectors, Jesus invites himself to dinner at Zacchaeus's house. People grumble, "He has gone to be the guest of one who is a sinner" (Luke 19:7). They fail to realize that Jesus has come "to seek out and to save the lost" (19:10). That is, in fact, exactly what Jesus does here, because Zacchaeus repents and says to Jesus, "Look, half of my possessions, Lord, I will give to the poor; and if I have defrauded anyone of anything, I will pay back four times as much" (19:8). Jesus responds, "Today salvation has come to this house" (19:9). Zacchaeus did not just say that he was sorry. Jesus' love for him caused him to change the direction of his entire life. That is what repentance is: responding to God's love and reorienting our lives in love and service to God.

God's call on our lives demands a response. We can say yes to God, accepting the salvation that we have through Jesus Christ, or we can say no to God and go about our business as usual. This decision, though, has real consequences. When we repent, when we say yes to God, we receive God's *justifying* grace. The word *justification*, as Wesley used it, means that God forgives all of our sins and that we have total acceptance by God. It does not matter who you are or what you have done in the past, no matter how badly you may think you have lived, God forgives you, and God accepts you. Again, the words of Paul come to mind: "neither death, nor life, nor angels, nor rulers, nor things present, nor things to come, nor powers, nor height, nor depth, nor anything else in all creation will be able to separate us from the love of God in Christ Jesus our Lord" (Rom 8:38-39).

To be clear, though, we *can* say no to God. We can live apart from God, now and forever. While some Christians through the centuries have been *universalists*, meaning that everyone will be saved regardless of how they have lived, this was not Wesley's perspective. Wesley believed that our lives here have real consequences for our eternal lives. We can reject the good life that is ours through God. Christians through the centuries have believed that being apart from God eternally is a terrible fate. The biblical writers use images of fire and darkness at times to talk about this state. For example, in the Gospel of Matthew Jesus sometimes refers to the "outer darkness, where there will be weeping and gnashing of teeth" (see 8:12; 22:13; 25:30). Jesus adds to this the image of a "furnace of fire" (see 13:42, 50). In other places, Jesus uses the image of *Gehenna*, often translated as *hell* in English Bibles (see Mark 9:43, 47). Gehenna was a real place in Jesus' day—the Hinnom Valley, located just outside of Jerusalem. This was a place where the worship of other gods, and even child sacrifice, had taken place. It was an unclean place, and therefore the people in and around Jerusalem used it as a garbage dump. Piles of burning trash, flames, stench, wild dogs snapping their teeth—this is what it is like, Jesus says, when you reject the good life that God has for you. It is like throwing your life on a garbage heap. New Testament writers use other images as well, such as the "lake of fire" in the book of Revelation (20:14-15). Not all of these images are meant to be taken literally. Biblical writers often use poetic, figurative language to express ideas that are really beyond our ability to understand. Nevertheless, these images are to be taken seriously. They teach us the difference between accepting God and rejecting God.

If we say yes to God at the same time that we receive God's justifying grace, however, we begin to receive God's *sanctifying* grace. This is what Wesley meant when he talked about being *born again*, a term that Christians have taken from Jesus' discussion with the teacher Nicodemus in John 3. Sanctifying grace is the work of the Holy Spirit that changes us from the inside out. Another term that Wesley used for this is *regeneration*. We are made new by the Holy Spirit. As Paul puts it, "If anyone is in Christ, there is a new creation" (2 Cor 5:17). Put differently, when the Holy Spirit comes into your life and begins to change you, a real change takes place. You begin to become a new kind of person, with different ideas, wishes, hopes, and goals. Wesley talked about the way in which the love of God pushes out the "love of the world, the love of pleasure, of ease, of honour, of money; together with pride, anger, self-will, and every other evil temper."[4] This is what Wesleyans mean when we talk about *holiness*: God's work in changing us, giving us hearts and minds that naturally do God's will, rather than rebel against it.

It is important to remember that sanctification (or regeneration), this process by which we become holier, more Christlike people, is a gradual one. It is generally not the case that, at the moment we repent of our sins and accept Christ into our lives, we will live a sinless existence. Rather, we grow in the faith. We grow in our love for God, our understanding of God and the Christian life, our desire to live as God would have us live, and our ability to live in that way. The goal is that our will becomes one with God's. The theologian Edwin Hatch expressed this desire for God's sanctifying grace in his hymn, "Breathe on Me, Breath of God," the first line of which goes:

> Breathe on me, Breath of God, fill me with life anew / that I may love what thou dost love, and do what thou wouldst do.[5]

With God's help, however, we can reach a point whereby we do live without sinning. At least, we do not sin intentionally. Wesley called this *Christian perfection* or *entire sanctification*. Wesley did *not* mean that we become perfect in the sense that we are free from error, mental or physical disabilities, or temptation. Rather, he simply meant that the Holy Spirit can work within us to such an extent that we no longer *willfully* sin. Our wills align with God's will. First Peter urges readers to live "for the rest of your earthly life no longer by human desires but by the will of God" (4:2). This was what Wesley meant by perfection. Yes, we can make mistakes, but we will not purposely and knowingly defy God. Christian perfection might sound like a tall order. After all, we tell one another that nobody is perfect. But perfection only makes sense if we remember that it is God's doing, not our doing. It is living out Jesus' instruction, "Be perfect . . . as your heavenly Father is perfect" (Matt 5:48). We should have faith in God and fully expect that the Holy Spirit will work this miracle within each of us who puts his or her faith in Jesus Christ.

Salvation has much to do with how we live in the here and now, but that is not the whole of it. Salvation also means that we will live with God forever in the resurrection. Through our faith in Jesus Christ and through our baptism, we enter into God's family. Through our faith in Jesus Christ we receive the powerful work of the Holy Spirit, God gives us new life, and this new life continues forever. Our eternal life with God is a continuation of our present life with God. This eternal life with God is not a disembodied, entirely spiritual existence. It is a new kind of *bodily* existence. The Christian hope is in the resurrection. We forget this sometimes, but Paul is clear: "this perishable body must put on imperishability, and this mortal body must put on immortality" (1 Cor 15:53). Paul teaches that there are both earthly bodies and heavenly bodies (see 1 Cor 15:40). He writes, "If there is a physical body, there is also a spiritual body" (15:44). After he was raised, Jesus had a real body, but it was a different kind of real body (see the discussion of this in chapter 2). Just as Jesus was raised from the dead, so also we who love and follow Jesus will be raised from the dead. In other words, Jesus' resurrection points forward to our own, a time when Christ will return and the dead in Christ will be raised. When the resurrection will happen no one knows, but that it *will* happen is assured to us through our faith in Jesus Christ.

A Lived Faith

From a practical side, what do we have to do to be saved, and how is it that we can grow in grace? As for the first question, to be saved, we must: (1) respond to God's call to repentance, (2) confess that Jesus Christ is Lord, and (3) put our faith (trust) in God for our present and future. When we do these things, the proper thing for us to do is to be baptized, if we have not been baptized already. Baptism is not only a way of receiving the Holy Spirit, but also a ritual whereby we enter into God's household. If we have already been baptized and have come to a mature faith as young people or adults, we should renew and reaffirm our baptisms within the church.

But what about after we are baptized (or have reaffirmed our baptism)? What happens then? After we make a decision to repent and to follow God, we should continue to grow in grace. Wesley suggested two ways of doing this: piety and mercy.[6] The term *piety* simply refers to things we do that help us draw closer to God. Wesley suggested prayer, both public and private; receiving Holy Communion; reading, hearing, and meditating upon the Scriptures, and fasting. One way to think about these kinds of actions is as spiritual exercises. We need physical exercises for our physical well-being, and we need spiritual exercises for our spiritual well-being. Another way to think about them is as instruments in God's medical bag. Through these instruments, we receive the healing balm of the Holy Spirit, and we are healed of the effects of sin.

Another way to continue to grow in the faith is through what Wesley called "works of mercy," which might also be called works of love and justice. Among these Wesley lists "feeding the hungry, clothing the naked, entertaining the stranger, visiting those that are in prison, or sick or variously afflicted." He also lists teaching people who are uneducated, bringing the good news of Jesus Christ to people who do not know him, and strengthening people who are being tempted to sin. We can surely add to this list many other items. In our own day, issues of extreme global poverty, HIV/AIDS, drug addiction, and other widespread crises make the Church's works of mercy and justice as crucial as they ever have been. There is no shortage of opportunities for us to engage in good works to which we are led by the Holy Spirit. These kinds of activities can be just as spiritually enriching as the works of piety. They are ways of living out God's will in the world, and they draw us closer to God and other people.

A Deeper Faith

We often hear people say that Jesus died for our sins. It is a commonplace Christian belief, but what does it mean? This is a deep and difficult question that Christians have debated through the centuries. That Jesus' death on the cross somehow makes our salvation possible is a bedrock conviction of Christian faith. We call this the *doctrine of atonement.* Think of atonement as "at-one-ment." The relationship between God and humans has been damaged by sin, and Christ, particularly through his death on the cross, heals that damage, making us one again. This is the idea behind one of the most often quoted passages of the New Testament: "In Christ God was reconciling the world to himself" (2 Cor 5:19). Exactly *how* Jesus' death reconciles us to God is what Christians have debated. Of course, we do not have to know exactly how something happens to agree that it does happen. For example, you might fly on an airplane with only the vaguest idea of the laws of aerodynamics.

The basic idea of Christian atonement, however, is this: human beings have sinned against God. When we hurt other people, that relationship has to be repaired. The same is the case with God: our damaged relationship with God has to be healed. We ourselves, however, cannot heal this relationship. We simply do not know how. Sin runs too deep. It is too widespread. God, therefore, has taken the initiative to come to us.

The Christian philosopher Eleonore Stump tells a story that helps us understand this. She writes of a mother, Anna, who has a young son, Nathan. Nathan, while playing soccer, carelessly destroys Anna's much-loved flower bed, despite her admonition that he not play soccer near her flowers. He utters a hasty apology, but the apology does not restore the flower bed, nor does it restore his mother's hurt feelings. Not only did she love the flowers, but she also feels that Nathan does not care for her feelings or wishes. As Stump puts it, "So what Nathan has done has created some distance between himself and his mother. His will and hers are not in harmony and he does not love her as he might; and her recognition of both of these facts makes her sad."[7]

Now, suppose that Nathan comes to a realization of the way in which he has hurt his mother. If he is truly sorry, he may in fact attempt to restore the flower bed, but he is too young to provide any real help. He cannot undo what he has done. If Nathan had someone to ask for help such as a big brother, the two of them might be able to combine their efforts and repair the damage. Even if his brother does most of the work, Nathan's desire to make right his wrong may restore the relationship between him and his mother. Nathan does not have a big brother, though, or anyone who can help him repair what he has destroyed.

Suppose, however, that Nathan is not sorry. He does not realize the damage he has done, and he shows not a care for his mother's feelings. His mother, then, will have to repair the flower bed entirely herself, doing the work that Nathan should be doing, in a sense, enduring his punishment for him, otherwise, the flower bed will simply remain in ruins. Seeing his mother do this work that he himself should do, however, might just cause Nathan to realize what he has done wrong and move him to repent of his actions. At that point, he might add his efforts to hers, attempting to work alongside her in the act of repairing the flower bed. In fact, he might not help very much, but his willingness to help, his desire to make things right, and his demonstrated love for his mother would make it possible for the two of them to be reconciled. The flower bed is thus repaired and the relationship is restored.

That is much like God's work in the Incarnation for us. God came to us in Jesus Christ to repair our broken relationship. We ourselves are incapable of so great a task, and so God, in Jesus Christ, took this work upon himself. The work was painful, and Christ did not deserve such agony, but he did this in order to allow the wrongs of sin to be righted again. Christ has atoned for our sins. He has made us "at one" with God, and we can come alongside Christ's work for us by repenting of our sins and working to make the wrongs in this world right again. We can never do what Christ did, but we can add our own, imperfect efforts to his.

The Catechism

Q. How does God reach out to sinful humans?

A. The Holy Spirit unceasingly calls us to repentance.

> "I am confident of this, that the one who began a good work among you will bring it to completion by the day of Jesus Christ" (Phil 1:6).

Q. What do we call this invitation to repentance?

A. We call it prevenient grace.

Q. Can we reject God's call to repentance?

A. Yes. We have free will.

Q. What is repentance?

A. It is a recognition that we have acted wrongly before God, and a desire to live according to God's will.

> "Let me hear joy and gladness;
>
> > let the bones that you have crushed rejoice" (Ps 51:8).

> "I have sent to you all my servants the prophets, sending them persistently, saying, 'Turn now everyone of you from your evil way, and amend your doings, and do not go after other gods to serve them, and then you shall live in the land that I gave to you and your ancestors.' But you did not incline your ear or obey me" (Jer 35:15).

"Now I rejoice, not because you were grieved, but because your grief led to repentance; for you felt a godly grief, so that you were not harmed in any way by us. For godly grief produces a repentance that leads to salvation and brings no regret, but worldly grief produces death" (2 Cor 7:9-10).

Q. What happens if we accept God's call to repentance and accept Jesus Christ?

A. Two things: justification and regeneration.

"[Christ] was handed over to death for our trespasses and was raised for our justification" (Rom 4:25).

"For his sake I have suffered the loss of all things, and I regard them as rubbish, in order that I may gain Christ and be found in him, not having a righteousness of my own that comes from the law, but one that comes through faith in Christ, the righteousness from God based on faith" (Phil 3:8-9).

"He is the atoning sacrifice for our sins, and not for ours only but also for the sins of the whole world" (1 John 2:2).

Q. What is justification?

A. It means that, through our faith in Jesus Christ, our sins are forgiven, and we are accounted righteous before God.

"Therefore, since we are justified by faith, we have peace with God through our Lord Jesus Christ. . . . Therefore just as one man's trespass led to condemnation for all, so one man's act of righteousness leads to justification and life for all" (Rom 5:1, 18).

Q. What is regeneration?

A. It is the renewal of human beings in righteousness through Jesus Christ, by the power of the Holy Spirit, whereby we are made partakers of the divine nature and experience newness of life.

> "So if anyone is in Christ, there is a new creation: everything old has passed away; see, everything has become new!" (2 Cor 5:17).

> "Clothe yourselves with the new self, created according to the likeness of God in true righteousness and holiness" (Eph 4:24).

Q. What is the effect of regeneration?

A. We are enabled to serve God and live as God would wish. This is also called sanctification.

> "Jesus answered, 'Very truly I tell you, no one can enter the kingdom of God without being born of water and Spirit. What is born of the flesh is flesh, and what is born of the Spirit is Spirit'" (John 3:5-6).

> "How can we who died to sin go on living in it? Do you not know that all of us who have been baptized into Christ Jesus were baptized into his death?" (Rom 6:2-3).

Q. Is it possible to live without willfully sinning?

A. Yes, this is called entire sanctification. It is a state of perfect love.

"Since we have these promises, beloved, let us cleanse ourselves from every defilement of body and of spirit, making holiness perfect in the fear of God" (2 Cor 7:1).

"He chose us in Christ before the foundation of the world to be holy and blameless before him in love" (Eph 1:4).

"He has now reconciled in his fleshly body through death, so as to present you holy and blameless and irreproachable before him" (Col 1:22).

"May the God of peace himself sanctify you entirely; and may your spirit and soul and body be kept sound and blameless at the coming of our Lord Jesus Christ" (1 Thes 5:23).

"Therefore Jesus also suffered outside the city gate in order to sanctify the people by his own blood" (Heb 13:12).

Q. What is the end of our salvation?

A. We will be raised from the dead and live eternally with God.

"When Christ who is your life is revealed, then you also will be revealed with him in glory" (Col 3:4).

"For the Lord himself, with a cry of command, with the archangel's call and with the sound of God's trumpet, will descend from heaven, and the dead in Christ will rise first. Then we who are alive, who are left, will be caught up in the clouds together with them to meet the Lord in the air; and so we will be with the Lord forever" (1 Thes 4:16-17).

"Then I saw a new heaven and a new earth; for the first heaven and the first earth had passed away, and the sea was no more" (Rev 21:1).

"And I heard a loud voice from the throne saying, 'See, the home of God is among mortals. He will dwell with them; they will be his peoples, and God himself will be with them'" (Rev 21:3).

Q. What happens if we reject God's gift of salvation?

A. The consequence of rejecting God's grace is separation from God, which the Bible sometimes calls "hell," "Gehenna," or "Hades."

"Then he will say to those at his left hand, 'You that are accursed, depart from me into the eternal fire prepared for the devil and his angels'" (Matt 25:41).

"If your hand causes you to stumble, cut it off; it is better for you to enter life maimed than to have two hands and to go to hell, to the unquenchable fire" (Mark 9:43-44).

"And the sea gave up the dead that were in it, Death and Hades gave up the dead that were in them, and all were judged according to what they had done. Then Death and Hades were thrown into the lake of fire. This is the second death, the lake of fire; and anyone whose name was not found written in the book of life was thrown into the lake of fire" (Rev 20:13-15).

In Your Own Words

1. God offers us prevenient grace, which is a hallmark of Wesley's teaching. Take a few minutes and write a definition of prevenient grace. Compare your definition with those of the rest of the class and come up with a class definition.

2. Saying yes to God can mean saying no to other things. What kinds of things does a Christian who has said yes do? How can other people know that we are saying yes to God? How do you understand your salvation? How do you talk about it with others?

3. If justification is total acceptance by God, how does knowing that we are totally accepted and loved by God affect our personal relationships with self and others (family, friends, strangers, rivals, enemies)?

4. What do you believe about hell? Who goes? Who doesn't? Does everyone get saved in the end?

5. As we grow in Christ and reflect him more completely, we become holier. We become sanctified, which is a process of growing in faith. Who are some of the saints of the faith that you know? Are there some people in your church whom you look up to for spiritual guidance? What would be the characteristics of a person who reflects Christ in all they do?

6. What are some acts of piety that might help you on your spiritual journey?

7 What Is the Church?

A Wesleyan Faith

When he and his colleagues established Methodism, John Wesley introduced a distinctive vision of church life. He turned church life into that of a family marked by warm fellowship. He created little churches within the bigger parish churches of his day. To be a Methodist was to be a member of a society, then to be a member of a small class of about a dozen, and, in the earliest days, then to be a member of a small band of six or seven brothers or sisters where one shared the most intimate details of one's life in strictest confidence. Wesley was not original in exploring small groups as pivotal in fostering genuine faith among believers. Other groups were also experimenting along these lines in England and on the continent of Europe. After his liberating experience of the Holy Spirit at Aldersgate, he spent several months observing how small groups worked among some German Christians called Moravians. In the network of small groups set up by Wesley, one learned to pray, to sing, to listen, to speak, to encourage, to respect others, and (in many cases) to lead. One was rooted in a family of serious believers and introduced to the great joy of Christian fellowship. One belonged to a small church within the bigger, local parish church. Belonging to a small group showed that one mattered as a person, as the unique individual that one is; belonging to the bigger local church within the national Church showed that one was part of something grander and even global.

There are churches, and then there is the Church. Churches (with a lower case *c*) are individual communities of Christians or buildings in which people worship. When we talk about the Church (with a capital *C*), however, we are talking about the community of all Christians everywhere, throughout the world and through all time. The Letter to the Hebrews speaks of our being surrounded by a "great . . . cloud of witnesses" (12:1). Christians are not lone rangers. We carry with us the faith and witness of untold numbers of believers who have followed Jesus Christ through the ages. Like they did, we carry the faith forward for untold numbers of believers who are to come. We have a great responsibility laid upon us, having been charged with proclaiming the gospel message to future generations.

In the Nicene Creed, a statement of faith written in the fourth century that has long helped define the parameters of Christian belief, we read that the Church has four distinct marks: it is one, holy, catholic, and apostolic. Let's start with what it means for the Church to be one. Over the long history of our faith, Christians have divided from one another many times, often because of disputes over belief. Since the sixteenth century, this process has accelerated rapidly. There are Roman Catholics and Eastern Orthodox Christians, Lutherans, Baptists, Quakers, Presbyterians, Anglicans and Episcopalians, Seventh-Day Adventists, many different stripes of Wesleyans, Pentecostals, and many other kinds of Christians, including various groups who identify with no particular denomination. Nevertheless, though we may disagree on matters of faith, some of which are quite important, we all have one Lord, Jesus Christ. All Christians stand under the lordship of Jesus. The hymn "The Church's One Foundation," written by Samuel J. Stone, talks about the relationship between Christ and the Church in this way:

The Church's one foundation is Jesus Christ her Lord;
She is his new creation by water and the Word;
From heaven he came and sought her to be his holy bride;
With his own blood he bought her, and for her life he died.[1]

So while Methodists, Presbyterians, Pentecostals, and Roman Catholics may disagree with one another over particular important matters, we are all still Christians. For all of us, Jesus is Lord. In that sense, we are all one.

The Church is also holy. We are holy because God makes us holy. Jesus said, "Where two or three are gathered in my name, I am there among them" (Matt 18:20). We read in the book of Acts that at Pentecost, the birthday of the Church, God poured out the Holy Spirit on people gathered in Jerusalem.

And suddenly from heaven there came a sound like the rush of a violent wind, and it filled the entire house where they were sitting. Divided tongues, as of fire, appeared among them, and a tongue rested on each of them. All of them were filled with the Holy Spirit and began to speak in other languages, as the Spirit gave them ability. (Acts 2:2-4)

From the first days of the Church, the Holy Spirit has been with us, empowering us to do the work to which we are called by Christ. Yes, human beings are imperfect and we often sin, but the Holy Spirit works within us to make us new. We are a part of God's new creation, and therefore we are also holy insofar as God makes us holy.

The term *catholic* can be a bit confusing. When we use the word *Catholic* with a capital *C,* we are usually referring to the Roman Catholic Church, the world's largest Christian denomination (though other Christian groups use *Catholic* as part of their name). In the sense in which we are using it, though, the word *catholic* means "universal." God intends for the Church to reach throughout the world, and all who confess Jesus as Lord are part of the Church. The Church is not reserved for a single people, race, or nation. The Church is for all people. We have a responsibility, then, to further the work of the Church in reaching out to all people, offering them the love of God in Jesus Christ.

The catholic nature of the Church is closely related to its oneness. Once we succeed in reaching other people, regardless of how different they are from us, we unite with them in Christ. Another way of saying this is that all Christians are part of the "body of Christ." As Paul writes, "For just as the body is one and has many members, and all the members of the body, though many, are one body, so it is with Christ. For in the one Spirit we were all baptized into one body—Jews or Greeks, slaves or free—and we were all made to drink of one Spirit" (1 Cor 12:12-13). Christians in Africa, Nebraska, Vietnam, Mexico, Australia, Hawaii, England, or any other place we can think of all share a common bond as members of the body of Christ.

When we say that the Church is apostolic, we mean that the faith that we proclaim stretches back to the earliest followers of Jesus. An *apostle* was someone who had followed Jesus during his ministry, had witnessed the resurrection, and was chosen by the Holy Spirit to proclaim the message about Jesus (Acts 1:22). The Apostle Paul, however, is one important exception to this rule. Paul did not follow Jesus during Jesus' earthly ministry. In fact, Paul was an enemy of Christianity and a persecutor of Christians. As he was going about this business of attacking the Church, however, he had a vision and heard the voice of the risen Christ speaking to him. He was struck blind for three days, and when he regained his sight, he was baptized and became the most influential figure among the earliest Christians in the spread of Christianity. (See Acts 9 for one version of this story.)

When we refer to the Church as *apostolic*, we mean that the faith we proclaim dates back to these earliest Christian preachers. The notion of the apostolic faith has always been important for Christians. In the Letter to the Hebrews, we read of the message of faith that was "declared at first through the Lord," and was "attested to by those who heard him, while God added his testimony by signs and wonders and various miracles, and by gifts of the Holy Spirit, distributed through his will" (2:3-4). As early as the second century, Christians developed the Rule of Faith, a basic summary of the apostolic witness. Later formulations, such as the Apostles' Creed and the Nicene Creed (see chapter 9), demonstrate more development than the Rule of Faith, but proclaim the same basic message. We need not and should not reinvent the faith for every subsequent generation. Rather, we try to find new ways of expressing the ancient truths of our faith, to reach people with the time-honored message that has sustained so many Christians through the centuries. That faith is the apostolic faith.

A Lived Faith

Practically speaking, what does it mean to be part of the Church? When we accept Christ and are baptized, we enter into this "great cloud of witnesses." Being a part of the Church does not just mean that you are saved or that you have a new social group. It means that you are part of the group of people who confess that Jesus is Lord, that God has put a claim on your life, and that your life will never be the same again. It means that the Holy Spirit is at work within you, forming you into the kind of person God is calling you to be. It means that much of your life will be different, from the way in which you think about human life to the way in which you spend your money.

Christ did not come merely to create churches. Christ came to change the world, and we who are Christ's followers are to continue in his work. You may say, "But I can't change the world," and that may or may not be true. But ask yourself what fifty, or a hundred, or hundreds of thousands, or millions of people seeking after God's will in the world can do. God does not need each of us to be the savior of the world. Jesus Christ has already come for that reason. Our task as the Church is to seek after God's will and to be obedient to the leadings of the Holy Spirit. Your church may not be able to solve all of the world's problems, but can you be a compassionate presence where you live? You yourself may not be able to give a great deal to the church, but many people giving just a bit can make a great deal of difference. And while you may be sensitive to this or that short-coming, that part of your life that you wish you could change, each of us can be confident that the Holy Spirit is alive within us, at work to allow us to do more than we ever thought possible.

Therefore, as a member of the Church, we are to attend a congregation of believers, to contribute to the life of that congregation, read Scripture, pray, participate in the sacraments (see chapter 8), and pray for the Holy Spirit to make us into the kind of people God wishes us to be. When God works within us in this way, Christians can change the world, save lives, and engage in small and large works of compassion and justice. In other words, the world begins to look more like God would want it to.

Unfortunately, Christians do not always live out this idea. Many churches seem to be associations of relatively nice people who worship on Sunday morning, but whose lives as Christians do not extend beyond the walls of their church buildings. Toward the end of his life, after the Methodist movement had enjoyed great success in renewing faith in Christ across England and was making inroads in North America, Wesley wrote about his movement with a note of concern.

I am not afraid that the people called Methodists should ever cease to exist, either in Europe or America. But I am afraid, lest they should only exist as a dead sect, having the form of religion without the power. And this undoubtedly will be the case, unless they hold fast both the doctrine, spirit, and discipline with which they first set out.[2]

The fact that we gather together and go through the motions does not mean that we are living in the way that the Church should. We can have the *form* of true faith without the *power*. Therefore we must always remain hungry in our communities of faith for the power of the Holy Spirit who makes us new and stirs us into action, bringing works of love, compassion, and justice into the world.

Another way of thinking about this is to say that *all* Christians are to be ministers of their local church. Your ministry may be teaching Sunday school, visiting the sick, cooking lunches on Sundays, working with the poor, working with children or youth, maintaining the church building, keeping the books, or something else. A ministry is a service to God through the Church. Some Christians, however, are called to *ordained* ministry, which is a way of saying that they are set apart to perform specific tasks in the life of the Church. Most often these tasks include leading worship, preaching, performing baptism, and presiding over the Lord's Supper. Different traditions think about ordination in different ways, and the terminology can differ from tradition to tradition. For example, an *elder* in the Presbyterian tradition will mean something different than in the United Methodist tradition. Some traditions, such as Roman Catholics and Episcopalians, have priests, but Wesleyans do not. We generally refer to our ordained people as *ministers* or *pastors*, with some subdivisions of these categories, such as *elder* and *deacon*. How people are ordained and how that ordination is understood can vary quite widely, but most traditions identify a group of people who are set apart to perform certain functions that are seen as especially sacred in the lives of their congregations.

A Deeper Faith

A lot of people want Jesus but they do not want his body. They are excited about what Jesus has done and they admire the amazing impact of his life across the centuries. They love who Jesus is, that he is the savior of the world, and they are thrilled at the change he brought in their lives in terms of forgiveness, new life, and hope for the future. However, they cannot stand all the faults and the problems they see in the Church. Others want his body but do not want Jesus. They love the benefits that come from going to church. They love the fellowship, the wonderful weddings, the music, and the opportunities for making new friends. They like the good things the Church does for the poor and for society as a whole. They are glad that when they die they will be given a good funeral. However, they prefer to keep Jesus at arm's length. They do not want to get too close to Jesus in case it interferes with what they want to do. Hence one often finds a deep tension among those who follow Jesus: some want Jesus but reject the Church while others want the Church but reject Jesus.

Given that the Church is the body of Jesus, we do not get to make these choices. If we vote for Jesus and follow him, then we have to come to terms with life in his body. And if we accept the benefits of his body, we have to come to terms with the source of those benefits in Jesus. If we are patient, we will see how these really fit together beautifully. As we come to terms with Jesus, we discover what it means to see that he is truly raised from the dead. He is not a dead Jesus hidden in a book or locked in the past; he is present wherever two or three are gathered in his name, and he works in and through his body, the Church. As we come to terms with the good things the Church offers, we will see that they all stem from the action of Jesus both in his own lifetime and in his action through the Holy Spirit in and through the Church. We can start with the owner of the house and then explore the house; or we can start with the house and then explore the work of the owner.

As we mature in the faith, we can begin to appreciate the marvel that the Church is. It has survived across the years despite internal turmoil and external persecution. It gave birth to hospitals in the fourth century. It created the great universities of the medieval world and many church-related universities in the modern period. It has been the source of protest against all sorts of injustice and has championed the cause of the poor and needy when nobody else cared. It has always provided the means of grace that are so pivotal for a vibrant spiritual life. Think of what our lives and our culture would be like if there had been no Church across the centuries. We can all name the faults and terrible things that have been done in the name of the Church; we need to be as quick to name all the good it has brought to us as individuals and to our cultures.

We might think of the issue this way. We are indebted to a host of complex institutions. Consider what we owe to the military, to the medical profession, to our universities, to our businesses and industry, and to our civic institutions from the local to the national level. Yet none of these can supply what the Church does; they cannot introduce us to the truth about God and the marvel of the gospel. The Church is the most important institution in the world. This is true because of what it is in itself and because of what it does to foster and correct other vital institutions in society at large. We would be lost without it. One of the great blessings of the gospel is that we get to belong to the Church, to serve in its varied ministries, and to be nourished by its unique practices and resources.

The Catechism

The Church

Q. What is the Church?

A. The Church is the community of all true believers under the lordship of Christ.[3]

> "And I tell you, you are Peter, and on this rock I will build my church, and the gates of Hades will not prevail against it" (Matt 16:18).

> "So then you are no longer strangers and aliens, but you are citizens with the saints and also members of the household of God, built upon the foundation of the apostles and prophets, with Christ Jesus himself as the cornerstone. In him the whole structure is joined together and grows into a holy temple in the Lord; in whom you also are built together spiritually into a dwelling place for God" (Eph 2:19-22).

Q. How is the Church described in the Bible?

A. The Church is described as the body of which Jesus Christ is the head and of which all baptized persons are members.[4]

> "He is the head of the body, the church; he is the beginning, the firstborn from the dead, so that he might come to have first place in everything" (Col 1:18).

Q. Why does the Church exist?

A. The Church exists for the maintenance of worship, the edification of believers, and the redemption of the world.[5]

"For where two or three are gathered in my name, I am there among them" (Matt 18:20).

"And Jesus came and said to them, 'All authority in heaven and on earth has been given to me. Go therefore and make disciples of all nations, baptizing them in the name of the Father and of the Son and of the Holy Spirit, and teaching them to obey everything that I have commanded you. And remember, I am with you always, to the end of the age' " (Matt 28:18-20).

Q. What are the four marks of the Church?

A. The Church is one, holy, catholic, and apostolic.

Q. Why is the Church described as one?

A. The Church is one, because it is one Body, under one Head, our Lord Jesus Christ.[6]

"I have other sheep that do not belong to this fold. I must bring them also, and they will listen to my voice. So there will be one flock, one shepherd" (John 10:16).

"So we, who are many, are one body in Christ, and individually we are members one of another" (Rom 12:5).

"There is one body and one Spirit, just as you were called to the one hope of your calling, one Lord, one faith, one baptism" (Eph 4:4-5).

Q. Why is the Church described as holy?

A. The Church is holy, because the Holy Spirit dwells in it, consecrates its members, and guides them to do God's work.[7]

> "Husbands, love your wives, just as Christ loved the church and gave himself up for her, in order to make her holy by cleansing her with the washing of water by the word, so as to present the church to himself in splendor, without a spot or wrinkle or anything of the kind—yes, so that she may be holy and without blemish" (Eph 5:25-27).

Q. Why is the Church described as catholic?

A. The Church is catholic because it proclaims the whole faith to all people, to the end of time.[8]

> "But you will receive power when the Holy Spirit has come upon you; and you will be my witnesses in Jerusalem, in all Judea and Samaria, and to the ends of the earth" (Acts 1:8).

Q. Why is the Church described as apostolic?

A. The Church is apostolic, because it continues in the teaching and fellowship of the apostles and is sent to carry out Christ's mission to all people.[9]

> "And Jesus came and said to them, 'All authority in heaven and on earth has been given to me. Go therefore and make disciples of all nations, baptizing them in the name of the Father and of the Son and of the Holy Spirit, and teaching

them to obey everything that I have commanded you. And remember, I am with you always, to the end of the age'" (Matt 28:18-20).

Q. Who are the ministers of the Church?

A. All baptized Christians are ministers of the Church.

Q. What does this mean?

A. It means that all Christians represent Christ and his Church; bear witness to Christ wherever they may be; carry on Christ's work of reconciliation in the world; and take their place in the life, worship, and governance of the church.[10]

Q. What is the difference between the ministry of the laity and the ministry of the ordained?

A. The ordained are called to specific responsibilities in the life of the local church, such as leading worship and administering the sacraments. They receive authority to fulfill these responsibilities from a bishop.

"And one does not presume to take this honor, but takes it only when called by God, just as Aaron was" (Heb 5:4).

In Your Own Words

1. On a scale from one to ten (one being low and ten being high) how welcoming is your church? Do you have visitors? Do they come back? How do you welcome adults, children, infants?

2. In the Wesleyan tradition, we consider our churches connected to one another. How connected is your church to others in your denomination, your community, locally, globally?

3. What do we mean by saying that the Church is holy?

4. Can you recite the Apostles' Creed? The Nicene Creed? How do these creeds summarize our faith?

5. Christians in local churches are set apart in different ways; that is, we all have ministries and we all have callings. Talk about these different callings and how they apply to your local church. Is God calling to you now? How would you describe your ministry?

6. How might the world and your community be different if the Church and your church disappeared?

8 What Are the Sacraments?

A Wesleyan Faith

During a generation when the Bishop of Oxford was trying to get his clergy to add a fourth celebration of the Lord's Supper to those observed at Christmas, Easter, and Whitsuntide (Pentecost), John Wesley was celebrating the Lord's Supper twice a week. There have been periods in the history of the Church when even its highest leaders celebrated the Lord's Supper only once a year. The revival led by the Wesleys, like an earlier revival in Scotland, involved an amazing rediscovery of the Lord's Supper as a vital means of grace. These services were so spiritually powerful that sometimes there could be as many as thirteen or fourteen hundred worshippers at one service. Imagine the challenge of ensuring that enough bread and wine were available on such occasions! John was convinced from firsthand testimony from those who attended these events that the Lord's Supper became a "converting ordinance," a place where people met the risen Lord for the first time and were never the same again. Charles Wesley wrote a marvelous collection of hymns that offer an amazing vision of Christ's mysterious, yet real, presence in the bread and the wine. Here is a stanza from one of them:

We need not now go up to heaven
To bring the long sought Saviour down;
Thou are to all already given,
Thou dost even now Thy banquet crown:
To every faithful soul appear,
And show Thy real presence here.

Think about the difference between knowing about a person and knowing a person. You may know where a person was born, where she lives, her address, the color of her eyes, and even her favorite movie, and still not really know her. Knowing a person involves a relationship. It involves interaction and communication. People who have never met face-to-face can still get to know one another, say, through social networking. Knowing a person is a much richer experience than knowing about a person. You cannot develop a friendship by simply knowing about a person. You certainly cannot develop a loving relationship in that way. Just as we get to know a person through such means as talking, messaging, writing, and spending time together, it is important that we also get to know God. It is not enough to know about God. Knowing about God is helpful only insofar as it helps you to get to know God. One of the main ways in which Christians have the opportunity to know God more fully is through the sacraments.

In Wesleyan traditions there are two sacraments: baptism and the Lord's Supper. The first of these we perform only once, the second again and again. The word *sacrament* comes from the same root as the word *sacred*. It is something that is set apart, something special within the life of faith. Why are the sacraments special? For one thing, they are outward signs of inward realities. In other words, they are symbols of the work that the Holy Spirit does within us. As a wedding ring is a symbol of the loving relationship between two people, the sacrament is a symbol of the loving relationship between

God and the believer. Even if we do not always perceive God's work in our lives—and indeed God often works subtly—they remind us that we love and serve a living God who is present with us, changing us into holier, more Christlike people.

Sacraments are much more than signs or reminders, though. Wesleyans believe that they are special "means of grace." Remember that a means of grace is a way of receiving the power and work of the Holy Spirit in our lives. Imagine that human beings are spiritually sick. We are in need of help. God is our physician, the Holy Spirit our medicine. Baptism and the Lord's Supper are time-honored, reliable ways of receiving the spiritual medicine that we so desperately need. In other words, we believe that God really does show up in the sacraments. While the minister leads us through the rituals of baptism or the Lord's Supper, and while we respond within the ritual, pray, and receive either water or the bread and cup, God does the most important work within the sacrament. Put in another way, the sacrament is not mainly about what we do, but about what God does. This is one reason Wesley believed that "it is the duty of every Christian to receive the Lord's Supper as often as he can."[1] (The other reason was that Christ commanded it.)

It is important to note that the sacraments are part of our life together, not just individually. We can pray by ourselves. We can read Scripture by ourselves. We cannot, however, baptize ourselves, nor can we partake of the Lord's Supper by ourselves. These acts are carried out in the community of other believers, and through these works we believe that God is at work in our community of faith. Even in cases where we bring the sacraments to homebound people, we see this as a way of their sharing in our worshiping life together. It is part of the nature of a sacrament to be carried out within the worshiping life of a community of believers.

The Greek word from which we get the word *baptism* simply means "to dip, plunge, or dunk." Baptism began as a kind of ritual bath. In fact, it was from the Jewish practice of taking ritual baths—baths that were supposed to cleanse people spiritually, rather than just physically—that the Christian practice of baptism emerged. Yet from the earliest days of the faith Christians have practiced baptism in a variety of ways. Some Christians believe that the only way in which a proper baptism can take place is by full immersion in water. Others believe that pouring or sprinkling water over the person being baptized is entirely acceptable. Among Wesleyans there are different ways of practicing baptism, and each of us learns these within our communities of faith. As a rule, though, baptism always involves water, it is carried out before a community of faith, and a minister normally performs the baptism. (And, yes, there are always exceptions.)

Regardless of how we practice baptism, though, there are some important concepts that we should have in hand as Wesleyans. Baptism is our initiation into the Church. In baptism, we enter into a covenant—a binding, sacred agreement—with God. We enter into God's household, adopted as God's children. In turn, God gives us new life by the power and work of the Holy Spirit. In some traditions, we can join a particular congregation of believers without having been baptized. We can certainly participate in worship, service, community, and other aspects of the life of the church without having been baptized. Baptism, however, means that we have entered into the Church catholic (universal), the community of all Christians who have ever lived, the household of God. It makes us part of something bigger than ourselves, that "great . . . cloud of witnesses" spoken of in Hebrews 12:1. As baptized people, we must order our lives in such a way as to be faithful to God, and we do so with the help and guidance of the Holy Spirit.

Baptism is not just a covenant but also a means of grace. It is a way in which we receive the power and work of the Holy Spirit. If our human nature has been corrupted by sin (see chapter 5), in baptism the Holy Spirit goes to work on us from the inside out and begins to restore the image of God within us. Can the Spirit do this without baptism? Of course. Like us, God has a free will, and God is not bound by our rituals or prayers. Nevertheless, we believe that baptism is a reliable way of bringing people into a closer relationship with God and invoking the Holy Spirit to be at work in the life of the baptized person.

If we see baptism as an initiation into the Church, a covenant, and a means of grace, we can see why many Wesleyans baptize infants. Christian parents who believe in this practice wish for their children to be a part of the Church from their earliest days, to be in covenant with God, and to receive God's healing grace. Of course, infants cannot decide for themselves if they wish to be baptized. Some Christians believe that baptism should come only after a person has made a conscious decision to follow Christ, so they do not baptize infants and young children. For those who do, however, the covenant is between the parents, the church, and God on behalf of the child. Since God is the primary agent in baptism, the child need not assent to entering the Church (being adopted into God's household) or receiving God's grace. These are loving gifts from God.

Whenever we baptize people, we baptize them in the name of the Father, Son, and Holy Spirit. To be baptized in the name of the Father, Son, and Holy Spirit means that we enter into a covenant of faithfulness to the Holy Trinity. We belong to the Trinity, are a part of God's household, and the Trinity is the only God whom we will worship. Early in the history of the Church, people baptized in the name of Jesus (see, for example, Acts 2:38; 8:16; 19:5). In time, however, Christians developed a more robust understanding of the work of God, and came to understand the significance of baptism in the name of the Holy Trinity. Baptism in the name of the Father, Son, and Holy Spirit is in fact what Jesus commands at the end of the Gospel of Matthew (28:19).

The Lord's Supper is also sometimes called *Holy Communion,* and sometimes called the *Eucharist* (a word that means "thanksgiving"). It involves a ritual in worship in which we eat bread and drink wine (though Wesleyans normally substitute unfermented grape juice). In this sacrament, we remember and give thanks for what Christ has done for us. Most often when we celebrate the Lord's Supper, the minister will recite the "Words of Institution." These are words that Jesus said on the night before he died on the cross. We read of these words in the Gospels of Matthew, Mark, and Luke, though the earliest account that we have of them comes from the Apostle Paul in 1 Corinthians 11:23-26:

> For I received from the Lord what I also handed on to you, that the Lord Jesus on the night when he was betrayed took a loaf of bread, and when he had given thanks, he broke it and said, "This is my body that is for you. Do this in remembrance of me." In the same way he took the cup also, after supper, saying, "This cup is the new covenant in my blood. Do this, as often as you drink it, in remembrance of me." For as often as you eat this bread and drink the cup, you proclaim the Lord's death until he comes.

This is why, when we receive the bread during communion, the person serving it says to us something like, "The body of Christ, broken for you," and when we receive the cup, "The blood of Christ, shed for you." The server is remembering the words Jesus said on the night on which Judas, one of his followers, betrayed him.

Like baptism, though, the Lord's Supper is not simply a remembrance. It is also a means of grace, a way in which we come to know and love God more fully by the power of the Holy Spirit. Roman Catholic and Eastern Orthodox Christians believe that the bread and the wine actually become the body and blood of Christ when the minister (priest) prays over them. They may still look like and taste like bread and wine, but they are in fact Christ's flesh and blood. Though we respect these brothers and sisters in the faith, Wesleyans have a different understanding of what happens to the bread and the wine. We believe that Christ really is present, though the essence of the bread and wine remains the same. When the minister prays over the bread and wine, the Holy Spirit makes Christ really present for us. Then, like spiritual medicine, Christ goes to work on our hearts, healing them of everything that can separate us from God. Just as with baptism, then, the Lord's Supper is mainly about what God does, not what we do. It is God's work in the Lord's Supper, not the work of the minister, the server, or the recipient, that is most important.

A Lived Faith

Through baptism and the Lord's Supper, we enter into covenant with God and grow in our relationship with God. Partaking of these sacraments is part of what it means to live in the Holy Spirit. Yes, prayer is important, as are Bible study and devotional time. Nevertheless, God has given to us through the Church these two special means of grace in order to lead us more deeply into a relationship with God. When we accept Christ, then, it really is important that we are baptized. It is equally important as we progress in our journey of faith that we nourish our souls with the Lord's Supper. Wesley said of this:

In this world we are never free from temptations. Whatever way of life we are in, whatever our condition be, whether we are sick or well, in trouble or at ease, the enemies of our souls are watching to lead us into sin. And too often they prevail over us. Now when we are convinced of having sinned against God, what surer way have we of procuring pardon from him than the "showing forth the Lord's death," and beseeching him, for the sake of his Son's sufferings, to blot out all our sins?[2]

Nevertheless, we should approach the communion table with humility and reverence. Remember: human beings have free will. We can accept the grace that we receive from the Holy Spirit, or we can reject it. We can allow God to change our lives, or we can refuse to do so. But if we consistently refuse to do so, and we come to the communion table, then we receive the Lord's Supper unworthily. The Apostle Paul addresses a problem of this nature in the church in Corinth. At that time, the Lord's Supper was a meal, not just bread and wine. The wealthy people in the congregation were feasting and getting drunk, while the poor people in the congregation did not have enough to eat. Paul asks them, "What! Do you not have homes to eat and drink in? Or do you show contempt for the church of God and humiliate those who have nothing?" (1 Cor 11:22). He tells them that when they eat the Lord's Supper in this way, they are doing so unworthily, and therefore they "eat and drink judgment against themselves" (1 Cor 11:29). The grace that we receive from God should make a difference in our lives. Christ did not die so that we could go along living the same way as before. Communion, moreover, is not a way of receiving forgiveness again and again when we are unrepentant of our sins. If we come to the table again and again to receive that grace, but again and again we reject it, Jesus is still present with us, but his presence may be as judge, rather than as savior.

A Deeper Faith

The sacraments have at times been a source of intense conflict across the centuries among Christians. Should we expand their number from two to seven? What are the exact conditions that make a sacrament valid and effective? Happily, the debate about numbers has become less heated of late. Everybody agrees that baptism and the Lord's Supper have a special place in the life of the Church. They go right back to Jesus, and from experience we know that they are indeed means of grace. God has promised to meet us in these practices. However, all also agree that God meets us in other practices. In preaching we hear the word of God; in fellowship together in the church we experience the Spirit; in services of ordination we ask God to come and equip those ordained to do the work God has called them to do. The reality of divine grace and action through a varied set of practices was known as a reality before we tried to nail it all down. There is an element of mystery we should not evade or explain away with our theories.

This does not mean we send our brains on a holiday and stop thinking about what is going on. It is right to ask searching questions about what exactly a sacrament is and sort out how to distinguish a sacrament from other things we do in our relationship with God. Otherwise we lose any real sense of their importance and approach them causally. Sacraments generally have two crucial elements: a material form, like water, bread, wine; and a spoken word, like "I baptize you in the name of the Father and of the Son and of the Holy Spirit." Hence they can be distinguished from other things that are a blessing in the life of the Church. Moreover, they are accompanied by the promise of God; God has made a covenant to meet us here. God's presence is secure regardless of the moral life of the one who administers them and regardless of our feelings. So, for example, we can be sure that when we come in repentance and faith that God really does meet us. Just as God worked in and through the material reality of Christ's body while he was here on earth, God now works through the material reality of water, bread, and wine.

Perhaps the most important truth about the sacraments is that it is the risen Christ who presides and gives grace at the sacraments. Of course, he works through human and earthly instruments, but he is also the One who is present. In the Wesleyan tradition that has led to a readiness to practice infant baptism and an insistence that all Christians be invited to the Lord's Table. Hence, even when children are baptized, Christ gives grace to them, a gift that does not depend on the feelings or even faith of the child. When we celebrate the Lord's Supper, the invitation is from the Lord, so that all who belong to him are invited to come and receive his grace here and now. This should not be confused with a lazy openness that ignores the need for genuine faith on the part of those baptized or that reduces the sacrament of the Lord's Supper to sentimental views of hospitality. If we accept that those present already belong to Christ and that their church is indeed a church, it would be strange to forbid them to come. Through the grace received at communion we can then draw closer together on church-dividing issues.

However, many Christians do not see things this way. Roman Catholic and Orthodox Christians see the Lord's Supper as the climax of our unity as Christians. They believe we should first achieve unity on the central matters of doctrine and practice before we have communion together. Catholics and Orthodox Christians worry about the carelessness they see in Protestantism. You can readily see that this conviction stems from a high view of the sacrament. Clearly we need patience and love to resolve these questions.

The Catechism

The Sacraments

Q. What is a sacrament?

A. It is a special means of grace and an outward sign of an inward reality.

Q. What are our two sacraments?

A. Baptism and the Lord's Supper.

Q. Who should administer the sacraments?

A. An ordained minister of the Order of Elders, unless none is present.

Q. What is baptism?

A. Baptism is a holy covenant with God by which we are brought into God's household and initiated into the life of the Church.

> "Jesus answered, 'Very truly I tell you, no one can enter the kingdom of God without being born of water and Spirit. What is born of the flesh is flesh, and what is born of the Spirit is spirit'" (John 3:5-6).

> "Peter said to them, 'Repent, and be baptized every one of you in the name of Jesus Christ so that your sins may be forgiven; and you will receive the gift of the Holy Spirit. For the promise is for you, for your children, and for all who are far away, everyone whom the Lord our God calls to him'" (Acts 2:38-39).

"As many of you as were baptized into Christ have clothed yourselves with Christ" (Gal 3:27).

"He saved us, not because of any works of righteousness that we had done, but according to his mercy, through the water of rebirth and renewal by the Holy Spirit. This Spirit he poured out on us richly through Jesus Christ our Savior, so that, having been justified by his grace, we might become heirs according to the hope of eternal life" (Titus 3:5-7).

Q. In whose name should Christians baptize?

A. In the name of the Father, Son, and Holy Spirit.

"Go therefore and make disciples of all nations, baptizing them in the name of the Father and of the Son and of the Holy Spirit, and teaching them to obey everything that I have commanded you" (Matt 28:19-20).

Q. How many times should a person be baptized?

A. Only once, as long as it is baptism in the name of the Father, Son, and Holy Spirit.

Q. Why is it wrong to baptize more than once?

A. Baptism is a holy covenant. Rebaptism demonstrates a lack of faith in the permanence of God's covenants.

Q. How should we baptize?

A. There are a variety of ways in which one may properly be baptized, including sprinkling, pouring, and immersion. One way is not more efficacious than the others.

Q. Should we baptize children?

A. Yes. Children of believing parents through baptism become the special responsibility of the Church. They should be nurtured and led to personal acceptance of Christ, and by profession of faith confirm their baptism.[3]

> "Keep these words that I am commanding you today in your heart. Recite them to your children and talk about them when you are at home and when you are away, when you lie down and when you rise" (Deut 6:6-7).

> "Train children in the right way, and when old they will not stray" (Prov 22:6).

> "Believe on the Lord Jesus, and you will be saved, you and your household" (Acts 16:31).

Q. What is the Lord's Supper?

A. The Lord's Supper is a ritual of communion with Christ and with other believers. It is also a remembrance of Christ's sacrifice on our behalf.

> "For I received from the Lord what I also handed on to you, that the Lord Jesus on the night when he was betrayed took

a loaf of bread, and when he had given thanks, he broke it and said, 'This is my body that is for you. Do this in remembrance of me.' In the same way he took the cup also, after supper, saying, 'This cup is the new covenant in my blood. Do this, as often as you drink it, in remembrance of me.' For as often as you eat this bread and drink the cup, you proclaim the Lord's death until he comes" (1 Cor 11:23-26).

"Then he took a cup, and after giving thanks he gave it to them, saying, 'Drink from it, all of you; for this is my blood of the covenant, which is poured out for many for the forgiveness of sins'" (Matt 26:27-28).

Q. Why do we call upon the Holy Spirit before receiving the Lord's Supper?

A. So that the Spirit will mediate Christ's presence to us in the bread and wine (juice).

Q. How is Christ present in the Lord's Supper?

A. Christ is really present in the Lord's Supper. His presence is a spiritual one.

"Those who eat my flesh and drink my blood have eternal life, and I will raise them up on the last day; for my flesh is true food and my blood is true drink. Those who eat my flesh and drink my blood abide in me, and I in them" (John 6:54-56).

In Your Own Words

1. If you have been baptized, share how, when, where. Did you grow up in the church? If so, share how you took communion growing up.

2. Talk about a meaningful communion time. How often do you prefer to take communion? Does communion nourish your soul? If not, how could it become more meaningful to you?

3. Sacraments mean that God is present in a special way. We see them as a means of grace. How do you understand this?

4. We talk about baptism as a holy covenant with God. What does this mean to you? Please put this into your own words. How do you talk about the meaning of baptism to your family and friends?

5. Some people celebrate the anniversary of their baptism. Is this something that you do or might find meaningful?

6. How is Christ present in the Lord's Supper for you?

9 What Are the Bible and Creeds?

A Wesleyan Faith

John Wesley famously called himself a "man of one book." Of course, the "one book" he referred to was the Bible. What is odd about this is that Wesley read all kinds of books. He was indeed deeply committed to reading the Bible and did so quite faithfully, but he read widely outside of the Bible as well. What he seems to have meant was that, of all the books that could be written, none compared to the Bible in importance. He believed very deeply that the Bible showed us the path to salvation in a way that no other book could, and that God worked through the Bible to lead us along that path. He wrote works called "Explanatory Notes" on both the Old and New Testaments because, while many works were written on Scripture for scholars and ministers, he wanted to make the Scriptures plain for the everyday person. Wesley cared about the Bible because he cared about salvation.

The question "What is the Bible?" is much harder than it sounds. At one basic level, Christians believe that the Bible is a work consisting of two major sections: the Old Testament and the New Testament. The Old Testament contains writings of the people of Israel before the time of Jesus. The New Testament contains writings from early Christians (say, within several decades of Jesus' death). The Old Testament contains thirty-nine books, though in Roman Catholic and Eastern Orthodox Bibles the Old Testament contains a few more than this. The New Testament for virtually all Christian traditions contains twenty-seven books. Together, the Old and New Testaments make up what is called the Christian *canon*.

The Bible is more than just a collection of writings, though. Christians believe that, through the Bible, God teaches us. This happens in a couple of different ways. First, we learn because Scripture teaches us truths that we would not know otherwise. The Bible teaches us about God's love for and work through Israel. It teaches us that Jesus Christ is the Son of God, and it recounts his teaching about God's will and ways. Further, it teaches us that Christ offers us salvation, that we should have faith in Christ, and that Christ will come again. It teaches us many other things as well. The bottom line is that we would not know these truths of the faith unless God revealed them to us, and God has chosen to do so through the Bible.

Further, though, God teaches us through the Bible by the work of the Holy Spirit. Wesley said that we should always close our reading of Scripture with prayer, so "that what we read may be written on our hearts."[1] Our Scripture reading should be a prayerful process, one in which we ask God to lead us into truth, and to change our hearts as we read. In other words, God helps us to read and interpret the Bible. This is not just the case with our individual readings, but in our readings as members of the Church. When we read the Bible, it is important to read in dialogue with other faithful readers. These readers can be members of our churches, parents, friends, or Christians of ages past who have written down their insights for us. We can learn from the ways in which God has led other believers to understand the Bible.

Though we do not always admit it, some parts of the Bible are more significant for us than for others. For example, take John 3:16: "For God so loved the world that he gave his only Son, so that everyone who believes in him may not perish but may have eternal life." Or take 1 John 4:8: "God is love." Another important passage for many Christians is Psalm 23, which begins, "The LORD is my shepherd, I shall not want." And then there are the Ten Commandments (see below in the catechism), found in Exodus 20:2-17 and Deuteronomy 5:6-21. Each of these passages helps us in a different way. John 3:16 tells of God's love for us, while 1 John 4:8 tells us of God's loving nature. Psalm 23 teaches us to trust in God, and the Ten Commandments give us a basis for living as God would wish. The Bible is a vast work, and it says and does many different things. While the entire Bible is important, some of what the Bible teaches has become central for our lives individually and together as Christians.

Along with the Bible, we also have *creeds*. A creed is a summary of basic Christian beliefs. The two most significant creeds of Christian faith are the Apostles' Creed and the Nicene Creed (see the catechism). Both of these creeds are old, written by Christian thinkers who knew the Bible and cared deeply about the content of the faith we proclaim. Creeds help us to keep our bearings as we think about God and God's work in the world. They help us remember that God is Father, Son, and Holy Spirit, and that this Holy Trinity has come to us in Jesus Christ and the Holy Spirit for our salvation. Put differently, the creeds teach us of the way in which God has acted to save us. They tell the story of our salvation through the Three Persons of the Trinity.

A Lived Faith

All too often, Bibles sit on shelves and collect dust. They do not work very well that way. For Bibles to work, we have to open them and read them. Just as important, we should read them prayerfully. Simply going through the motions is not enough. We should pray that God will enlighten us by the power and work of the Holy Spirit as we read, and that in so doing God will make us holier people.

For many people, though, reading the Bible can seem like a daunting task, if not an impossible one. Where does one start? At the beginning? It is pretty easy to get bogged down along the way: "Canaan became the father of Sidon his firstborn, and Heth, and the Jebusites, the Amorites, the Girgashites, the Hivites, the Arkites, the Sinites . . ." (Gen 10: 15). That's supposed to be spiritually enriching? What if we start in the New Testament? "Abraham was the father of Isaac, and Isaac the father of Jacob, and Jacob the father of Judah and his brothers, and Judah the father of Perez and Zerah by Tamar, and Perez the father of Hezron . . ." (Matt 1:2-3). No wonder so many people start reading the Bible with the best of intentions, but fail to stick with the task. There is incredibly rich material in the Bible, but at times it can be difficult to understand, or to see how the parts fit together, or to identify ways in which a particular passage relates to the life of faith. Especially if we are inexperienced readers, we need the help of more experienced readers to guide us through our Bible, which is a large and complex book. This is one of the advantages of being part of a Bible study. We can learn a great deal from the ways in which other people read Scripture, especially if those people have been reading and praying over the Scripture for a long time. One helpful series is called DISCIPLE. The first part of this series takes readers through the entire Bible. If you cannot find a good Bible study or your schedule will not allow it, it can be helpful to get a Bible with a reading plan that will take you through the Scriptures in a certain number of months or years. Reading the Bible can be a wonderful, life-giving experience, but no one said it would be easy.

It is important that Christians recite creeds together, especially during worship. The content of our faith really does matter, and by reciting creeds, we rehearse that basic content again and again. Churches are not just gathering places. They are communities of people who confess God's saving work through the Father, Son, and Holy Spirit. When we recite our creeds, we are reminded of our identity as a people of God, a people who believe in a saving, living God who is constantly at work within our midst. We are reminded that the past, present, and future are all God's, that God has saved, is saving, and will always save until heaven and earth are one.

A Deeper Faith

How should we think of God's role in the production of the Bible and the creeds? Does God inspire the Bible and then leave the Church to figure out what to believe by developing a creed? On this view, we should distinguish between the Bible, the word of God, and the creeds, the traditions of human agents. Or is the Holy Spirit at work inspiring the Church to develop both the Bible and the creeds? On this view, we receive both Bible and creeds as great gifts from God that have their own unique role to play in our spiritual maturity.

All serious Christians believe in God's self-revelation through the history of Israel and in the life, death, and resurrection of Jesus Christ. God really spoke to the people of Israel in the covenant with Abraham, through mighty acts of deliverance, through the words of the prophets; and God spoke even more powerfully and definitely in Jesus. So we do have a genuine word from God; and that word is made available in the Bible. We have special revelation. If this is so, then we can expect God to inspire those who received the word of God to preserve it, reliably interpret it, and make it available. This is clearly one reason why the Bible is crucial. It gives us access to divine revelation; we are not left to sort things out on the basis of mere reason or experience. God has provided an inspired account of what he has done to free us from sin and death.

However, there is more to the Bible than special revelation. We also see the response to that revelation, say, in the Psalms and in Wisdom literature. And we see believers wrestle with the meaning of divine revelation in the letters of the New Testament. God works in this process too, inspiring what we should think and do as we follow Christ. Such material forces us to wise up about our need for God, drives us to repentance, and helps us both understand and respond to the gospel. The most famous verse on biblical inspiration makes this clear (2 Tim 3:16). The purpose of the Bible is spiritual; it both informs our faith and builds up our faith. The inspiration of the Spirit works at the origination of the Bible and in the reception of the Bible here and now. Because of the work of the Spirit, the Bible is reliable in what it tells us about God and salvation and it is effective in bringing us to experience the word of God and grow in the wisdom of God.

Some Christians have wanted to go further and insist on the inerrancy or infallibility of the Bible in everything it intends to say. Wesley at times was drawn to this view. However, when explored to the full, it has created conflict with the best work we have in both history and science. Many have then lost their faith because they were promised more than the Bible delivers. It is much wiser and much more spiritual to see the Bible as both reliable in its giving us special revelation and in making us wise to the reality of salvation.

Equally, it is much better to see the Holy Spirit at work in every aspect of the Church's life, giving us not only a marvelous book that conveys the word and wisdom of God but also an in-depth summary of the heart of the faith in the great creeds of the Church. The creeds were written for those coming to baptism so that they could have a basic orientation in the faith. We can trace their origins to Scripture itself (1 Cor 15:1-6). It is surely strange to think that God would come to the world in Christ and save it at such cost and then refuse us help when we sought to provide a deep summary of the faith for those coming to baptism. The Spirit was at work throughout the life of the Church: in its witness, its preaching, its evangelism, its sacraments, in the choice of leaders, in the production and adoption of the Bible, and in the creation of the creeds. What makes the Bible unique is not its mode of production by the Spirit, but its role in providing us the word and wisdom of God that operates as a pivotal source and norm in the life of faith.

The Catechism

The Bible

Q. What do we mean by the Scripture?

A. The Holy Bible, the Old and New Testaments.

Q. What is the Old Testament?

A. The Old Testament is the part of our Bible that tells us of God's self-revelation to and through the Hebrew people.

> The Old Testament comprises the following thirty-nine books: Genesis, Exodus, Leviticus, Numbers, Deuteronomy, Joshua, Judges, Ruth, 1 Samuel, 2 Samuel, 1 Kings, 2 Kings, 1 Chronicles, 2 Chronicles, Ezra, Nehemiah, Esther, Job, Psalms, Proverbs, Ecclesiastes, the Song of Solomon, Isaiah, Jeremiah, Lamentations, Ezekiel, Daniel, Hosea, Joel, Amos, Obadiah, Jonah, Micah, Nahum, Habakkuk, Zephaniah, Haggai, Zechariah, and Malachi.

Q. What did God promise to the Hebrew people?

A. That they would be God's people, and that through them all nations would come to know the one true God.[2]

> "You shall not bow down to them or worship them; for I the LORD your God am a jealous God, punishing children for the iniquity of parents, to the third and the fourth generation of those who reject me, but showing steadfast love to the thousandth generation of those who love me and keep my commandments" (Exod 20:5-6).

Q. What response did God require of them?

A. To be faithful; to love justice, do mercy, and walk humbly with their God.[3]

> "He has told you, O mortal, what is good; and what does the LORD require of you but to do justice, and to love kindness, and to walk humbly with your God?" (Micah 6:8).

Q. Where in the Old Testament is God's will for us shown most clearly?

A. God's will for us is shown most clearly in the Ten Commandments.[4]

Q. What are the Ten Commandments?

A. They are the laws given to Israel through Moses (Exod 20:1-18; Deut 5:1-22).

"When God finished speaking with Moses on Mount Sinai, he gave him the two tablets of the covenant, tablets of stone, written with the finger of God" (Exod 31:18).

Q. What do we learn from the Ten Commandments?

A. We learn two things: our duty to God, and our duty to our neighbors.[5]

Q. Since we do not fully obey them, are they useful at all?

A. Since we do not fully obey them, we see more clearly our sin and our need for redemption.[6]

"For 'no human being will be justified in his sight' by deeds prescribed by the law, for through the law comes the knowledge of sin" (Rom 3:20).

"Anyone, then, who knows the right thing to do and fails to do it, commits sin" (James 4:17).

Q. What are the Ten Commandments?

A. There are two parts, the first and second tables:

The First Table (our duties toward God):
1. You shall have no other gods before me.
2. You shall not make for yourself an idol.
3. You shall not make wrongful use of the name of the LORD your God.
4. Observe the sabbath day and keep it holy.

The Second Table (our duties toward our neighbors):

5. Honor your father and your mother.

6. You shall not murder.

7. You shall not commit adultery.

8. You shall not steal.

9. You shall not bear false witness against your neighbor.

10. You shall not covet anything that is your neighbor's.[7]

Q. What is the New Testament?

A. The New Testament is the part of our Bible that tells us of God's definitive self-revelation through Jesus Christ, the Son of God; and the ministry of the apostles and other early followers of Jesus.

> The New Testament comprises the following twenty-seven books: The Gospel According to Matthew, the Gospel According to Mark, the Gospel According to Luke, the Gospel According to John, the Acts of the Apostles, the Letter to the Romans, the First Letter to the Corinthians, the Second Letter to the Corinthians, the Letter to the Galatians, the Letter to the Ephesians, the Letter to the Philippians, the Letter to the Colossians, the First Letter to the Thessalonians, the Second Letter to the Thessalonians, the First Letter to Timothy, the Second Letter to Timothy, the Letter to Titus, the Letter to Philemon, the Letter to the Hebrews, the Letter of James, the First Letter of Peter, the Second Letter of Peter, the First Letter of John, the Second Letter of John, the Third Letter of John, the Letter of Jude, and the Revelation to John.

Q. What does Jesus Christ promise us in the New Testament?

A. Christ promises to bring us into the kingdom of God and give us life in all its fullness.[8]

"While physical training is of some value, godliness is valuable in every way, holding promise for both the present life and the life to come" (1 Tim 4:8).

Q. What are the commandments taught by Christ?

A. Christ taught us the "Summary of the Law" and gave us the New Commandment.[9]

Q. What is the "Summary of the Law"?

A. " 'You shall love the Lord your God with all your heart, and with all your soul, and with all your mind.' This is the first and the great commandment. And the second is like it: 'You shall love your neighbor as yourself' " (Matt 22:37-40; Mark 12:30-31).[10]

Q. What is the New Commandment?

A. The New Commandment is that we love one another as Christ loved us.[11]

"Beloved, since God loved us so much, we also ought to love one another" (1 John 4:11).

"Love does no wrong to a neighbor; therefore, love is the fulfilling of the law" (Rom 13:10).

"In everything do to others as you would have them do to you; for this is the law and the prophets" (Matt 7:12).

"Put away from you all bitterness and wrath and anger and wrangling and slander, together with all malice, and be kind to one another, tenderhearted, forgiving one another, as God in Christ has forgiven you" (Eph 4:31-32).

Q. What is the purpose of the Scripture?

A. To lead us into salvation.

"From childhood you have known the sacred writings that are able to instruct you for salvation through faith in Christ Jesus" (2 Tim 3:15).

Q. How does Scripture lead us into salvation?

A. We receive the Holy Spirit in our prayerful reading of Scripture, and, with the help of the Holy Spirit, Scripture reveals the word of God so far as it is necessary for our salvation.[12]

"No prophecy ever came by human will, but men and women moved by the Holy Spirit spoke from God" (2 Pet 1:21).

"We also constantly give thanks to God for this, that when you received the word of God that you heard from us, you accepted it not as a human word but as what it really is, God's word, which is also at work in you believers" (1 Thes 2:13).

"All scripture is inspired by God and is useful for teaching, for reproof, for correction, and for training in righteousness, so that everyone who belongs to God may be proficient, equipped for every good work" (2 Tim 3:16-17).

The Creeds

Q. What are the creeds?

A. The creeds are statements of our basic beliefs about God.

Q. What are the two great creeds of the Church?

A. The two great creeds of the Church are the Apostles' Creed and the Nicene Creed.

Q. What is the Apostles' Creed?

A. The Apostles' Creed is the ancient creed of Baptism; it is used in the Church's worship to recall our baptismal covenant.[13]

Q. How do we recite the Apostles' Creed?

A. We recite it as follows:

I believe in God the Father Almighty,
  maker of heaven and earth.

And in Jesus Christ his only Son our Lord:
  who was conceived by the Holy Spirit,
    born of the Virgin Mary,
    suffered under Pontius Pilate,
    was crucified, dead, and buried; he descended into hell;
  the third day he rose from the dead;

he ascended into heaven,
    and sitteth on the right hand of God the Father Almighty;
from thence he shall come to judge the quick and the dead.

I believe in the Holy Spirit;
    the holy catholic church;
    the communion of saints;
    the forgiveness of sins;
    the resurrection of the body;
    and the life everlasting. Amen.[14]

Q. What is the Nicene Creed?

A. The Nicene Creed is the definitive statement of the Trinitarian faith.

Q. How do we recite the Nicene Creed?

A. We recite it as follows:

We believe in one God,
    the Father, the Almighty,
    maker of heaven and earth,
    of all that is, seen and unseen.

We believe in one Lord, Jesus Christ,
    the only Son of God,
    eternally begotten of the Father,
    God from God, Light from Light,
    true God from true God,

begotten, not made,

of one Being with the Father.

through him all things were made.

For us and for our salvation

    he came down from heaven,

    was incarnate of the Holy Spirit and the Virgin Mary

    and became truly human.

    For our sake he was crucified under Pontius Pilate;

    he suffered death and was buried.

    On the third day he rose again

    in accordance with the Scriptures;

    he ascended into heaven

    and is seated at the right hand of the Father.

    He will come again in glory

    to judge the living and the dead,

    and his kingdom will have no end.

We believe in the Holy Spirit, the Lord, the giver of life,

    who proceeds from the Father and the Son.

    who with the Father and the Son

        is worshiped and glorified,

    who has spoken through the prophets.

    We believe in one holy catholic and apostolic church.

    We acknowledge one baptism

        for the forgiveness of sins.

    We look for the resurrection of the dead,

        and the life of the world to come. Amen. [15]

In Your Own Words

1. Share your favorite Bible verse and story. Even if you do not know many, perhaps there is one in this book that has been meaningful to you.

2. Take some time and discuss your own understanding of how God speaks to you through the Bible. Does being part of a group help you in your own study? If so, how?

3. Do you have a regular Bible study time? Place? Method or plan? Group? Do you need greater access to study helps, for example Bible commentaries, Bible dictionaries? Share what resources you find helpful.

4. Do you believe it is important to memorize Bible verses? If so, what verses have you memorized? How do you use them to strengthen your faith?

5. Most people find some passages in the Bible difficult, worrisome, and troubling. Are there things or people in the Bible that trouble you?

6. Knowing the Bible helps shape us as Christians, but sharing the Bible stories with others transforms our daily living. What is the best way to share what the Bible means to you, to your family, to your friends, to your coworkers?

7. Take some time this week and read the creeds every day. Do you have a creed by which you live? What are your deepest convictions about God?

8. When you recite the creeds or even the Lord's Prayer, are you simply saying words or thinking about the meaning? Does your church give you an opportunity to say the creeds? How important is it to say the creeds in the church service?

10 How Should Wesleyans Live?

In this final chapter, we will depart from the format of preceding chapters. Every chapter so far has had a section called "A Lived Faith," in which we talked about practical living in light of the faith that Wesleyans claim. In this chapter, the entire focus will be on Christian living, and specifically on three rules that Wesley had for people within his communities of faith. For Wesley, being a Methodist was not just about going to church or saying the right words, though attending church and right belief were important to him. At its root, the Methodist movement was about being changed by the work of the Holy Spirit. As we have said many times in this book, Wesley believed that God worked within us to lead us to lives of holiness. So being a Methodist was—and still should be—as much about how one lives as it is about what one believes. Wesley's three basic rules for the people within his communities were: (1) do no harm, (2) do good, and (3) attend upon the ordinances of God. The first two are not as simple as they might seem, and the third is not as complicated as it sounds.

Do No Harm

Let's take the first one, "Do no harm." This could involve harm to ourselves or to others, or offense against God. Our actions have consequences. The way in which we speak to other people, our habits of spending money, the extent to which we yield to selfish temptations, and the ways in which we spend our time affect us personally, and they affect other people too. Think, for example, about how the words that we say can affect other people. Gossip, judgmental comments, insults, and insensitive remarks can wound people very deeply. They can destroy friendships and even break up marriages. Children may remember hurtful words of parents even years after the fact. The Letter of James (3:5-10) reminds us that the words of our mouths can have serious consequences:

> How great a forest is set ablaze by a small fire! And the tongue is a fire. The tongue is placed among our members as a world of iniquity; it stains the whole body, sets on fire the cycle of nature, and is itself set on fire by hell. . . . With it we bless the Lord and Father, and with it we curse those who are made in the likeness of God. From the same mouth come blessing and cursing. My brothers and sisters, this ought not to be so.

Of course, there are many other ways to do harm. Abuse of alcohol and drugs, the use of pornography, and gluttony may seem like they affect primarily the person who takes part in these acts, but their effects upon other people can be profound. Substance abuse, for example, can affect families for generations, wounding children who, when adults, may inadvertently wound their own children. The use of pornography contributes to a widespread industry that creates addiction, destroys lives, contributes to human trafficking, breaks up marriages, contributes to promiscuous sexual behavior, exploits women, and at times even exploits children. Gluttony (say, chronic overeating) can affect us in many ways, including the way in which we use money. It affects our health, which in turn affects our ability to engage in the work of Christian service. It can affect our lifespan, which comes to bear on the amount of time and quality of time that we spend with those we love. The bottom line is this: human beings are connected to one another in powerful networks of relationships. It is hard to identify any sins or crimes that affect only one person.

We can also harm ourselves and others by damaging our relationship with God. Wesley pointed out, for example, that we do harm when we use God's name wrongly, or when we neglect to observe the holy day of rest that God has set aside for us (the Sabbath). We harm ourselves because we create distance between ourselves and God. We may harm others by our failure to live out the faith that we proclaim. A life lived faithfully is a powerful witness to those who do not believe. A person who claims Christ but lives no differently than anyone else says to the world that Christians do not practice what they preach, and people are driven farther away from the faith. Likewise, we damage our relationship with God when we hurt our neighbors. We read in 1 John: 4:20-21:

> Those who say, "I love God," and hate their brothers or sisters, are liars; for those who do not love a brother or sister whom they have seen, cannot love God whom they have not seen. The commandment we have from him is this: those who love God must love their brothers and sisters also.

Of course, no one can live life without hurting other people at times. We often may not even realize that we are hurting others. The point though, is to live life mindful of the fact that life is not all about us. It is about God, other people, and the ways in which we relate to them. When we realize that we are bound up in this powerful network of relationships and that, whether we want them to or not, our actions do affect other people, we may begin to live differently. When we begin to live intentionally as God would have us live, the world begins to look more like God would have it look—and the best part is that we have the Holy Spirit to help us live as we should.

Do Good

Nobody really wants to be a goody-goody person. It smacks of arrogance and self-righteousness. However, when we come across real goodness we are delighted and drawn to it like a hungry person seeks out food when he or she smells it from afar. We also know that real goodness is deep and that it is costly to practice.

In thinking about goodness Wesley set a high bar; he developed a gold standard that frankly scares us if we take it seriously. It begins with a commitment to being merciful in every possible way. Happily, we can start exactly where we are, doing the best we can and becoming more and more merciful over time. This paves the way for doing good of every possible sort to every possible person, insofar as we have opportunity and insofar as it is possible. Again we start where we are with the opportunities before us and the options open to us, but the goal is to go deeper in our love for our neighbor and to extend that love to everybody. The love begins with the physical needs of people: feeding the hungry, clothing the naked, helping the sick, and visiting those in prison. It then extends to their spiritual needs: helping them find God by providing relevant information, by encouraging them in their journey, by clearing up confusion and error, and by showing them that by grace victory over evil is possible. In doing such good we should begin with those who are already in the Church or seeking to be part of it. The world takes care of its own, so Christians should begin by taking care of their brothers and sisters in need. Once we learn what it is to be good there, we can then expand the circle of care.

This kind of goodness cannot be had on the cheap. It requires being street-smart and prudent. We have to learn to discipline our desires and stop spending on unnecessary goods and trinkets. This can readily drive us to despair, so we have to be patient and work through our inevitable failures. We have to learn how to face up to ridicule and opposition, expecting to be disliked and even hated. This is a surprising turn of events. We expect folk to applaud those who do good. Happily, many do, for we admire those who share their money and lives with those who are needy. So why should we expect ridicule and opposition when we do good?

There are obvious reasons why this is so. First, this is a really deep goodness that goes beyond ordinary charity and giving to others. It is comprehensive and costly. Hence it can produce envy and jealousy. Second, it can lead folk to see how shallow their love is and provoke a sense of shame that translates into anger and accusation. This is a level of goodness that shows us how impoverished we can be in our giving. Third, this kind of goodness refuses to settle for mere physical or political acts of goodness and tackles the deep spiritual problems that we can see all around us. This can lead people to hold that those who are committed to this kind of goodness are arrogant, that they believe they are better than others. It can also lead some to feel guilty about how little they really care and drive them to strike out in scorn and in despair.

The deepest reason for opposition is hard for the average do-gooder to understand. Goodness like this comes only from God. On the one hand, we are so self-centered that many of our acts of kindness and goodness are self-serving; they are intended to make us feel good and look good. On the other hand, once we reach for this kind of goodness, we realize that only the grace and power of God can create and sustain it. We are shaken to the foundations and are now confronted with our sin and our bondage to our disordered desires. Yet this is a wonderful discovery because it forces us to come to terms with reality and to look for help from God. Happily, help is at hand, right here and now, in the means of grace given in the Church.

Attend upon the Ordinances of God

This one is a mouthful, but it is simpler than it sounds. The United Methodist bishop Reuben Job phrased it a bit differently: "Stay in love with God."[1] How do we do this? Like any relationship, we have to attend to our relationship with God. We cannot take it for granted. Wesley identified three practices that he felt were most important in this regard: prayer, "searching the Scriptures," and receiving the Lord's Supper.[2] We have discussed reading Scripture in chapter 9 and the Lord's Supper in chapter 8, and though we have talked about prayer many times in various chapters, it is worth spending a bit more time on here. Prayer matters and it makes a difference. We should commit every part of our life to God through prayer. Our jobs, families, money, talents, joys, opportunities, sorrows, and worries—we should give all of these to God in prayer. "That's a lot of praying," you may say, and indeed it is, but the Christian life is a life of prayer. Paul, in fact, tells us to "pray without ceasing" (1 Thes 5:17). Our prayers do not have to be elaborate, long, or drawn out. When Jesus' disciples asked him how they should pray, he taught them a simple prayer that we call the "Lord's Prayer" (Matt 6:9-13; Luke 11:1-4). It is recounted in two versions below in the catechism.

Not all of our prayers will be answered as we would wish. God is not a genie, granting our every wish, enslaved to our desires. God is the Lord of all creation, and by God's grace, we will receive gifts of the Holy Spirit. We may experience profound, life-changing miracles, while at other times we will experience disappointment and heartache. Yet even in these painful times, it is important to keep praying, if we can. Prayer can be a way of inviting God to share in our suffering, to comfort us and others who are hurting, to strengthen us so that we may reach a place of healing, and to guide us to respond to life's hardships in Christlike ways. Prayer is not always easy.

Sometimes the words do not come. Sometimes, just as in any relationship, we do not know what to say, or we are not in a frame of mind to listen. Prayer, nevertheless, is a crucial part of the Christian life.

Though not among the three most important practices that Wesley wrote about, another way in which we maintain our relationship with God is by attending public worship. As we worship together, we participate in community prayer and singing. We (hopefully) receive the Lord's Supper on a regular basis, and we affirm both our faith and the faith of others in the ritual of baptism. We hear the Bible read aloud before the community of believers, and we are led through the Scriptures in the sermon. Remember: being a Christian is not all about me. It is about being a part of the community of faith that comes together in praise, thanksgiving, and confession of sin, and that honors God by the life and witness of its members.

Christians through the centuries have engaged in many other practices as ways of growing closer to God. We often call these practices spiritual disciplines. One such discipline that Wesley engaged in was fasting, depriving oneself of food, or of certain foods, for a particular period of time. Of course, we have to be careful with fasting, and it is important that we know what we are doing before we begin. Nevertheless, this is a time-honored act of dedicating oneself to God. Another practice is meditation. We can meditate upon Scripture, a particular prayer, insights of Christian writers whose work is meaningful to us, or other material. Meditation can be hard work. It is in the nature of our minds to wander. Meditation, like fasting, really does take discipline, and you may have to work up to it. It can, however, be an effective way to center our minds on God and seek God's will for our lives. For more information on spiritual disciplines, see Richard Foster's book *A Celebration of Discipline: The Path to Spiritual Growth*.[3]

The Catechism

Wesleyan Living

Q. What is the first rule of a Wesleyan way of life?

A. To do no harm, avoiding evil of every kind.

> Wesley specifically singled out certain kinds of behavior, such as taking the name of God in vain, profaning the sabbath, fighting and quarrelling, taking what is not rightfully and morally ours, wasteful use of time, and the improper use of money.

Q. What is the second rule of a Wesleyan way of life?

A. To do good to all people as often as I am able, being merciful to the greatest extent that I am able.

> Wesley indicates that we should attend to the material and spiritual needs of other people, providing not only such goods as food and clothing, but also instruction, reproof, and exhortation as well. He also says that it is preferable for Christians to employ and do business with other Christians, because the world will take care of its own, but not those who follow Christ.

Q. What is the third rule of a Wesleyan way of life?

A. To attend upon all of the ordinances of God.

These include such practices as public worship, reading and preaching Scripture, partaking of the Lord's Supper, family prayer, private prayer, and fasting.

Q. What is prayer?

A. Prayer is an act of communion with God, which may include petitions, praise, or thanksgiving. Prayer may be silent or aloud.

"Do not worry about anything, but in everything by prayer and supplication with thanksgiving let your requests be made known to God" (Phil 4:6).

"O give thanks to the LORD, for he is good, / for his steadfast love endures forever" (Ps 136:1).

Q. In whose name should we pray?

A. We should pray in the name of Jesus, or in the name of the Father, Son, and Holy Spirit.

"Be filled with the Spirit . . . giving thanks to God the Father at all times and for everything in the name of our Lord Jesus Christ" (Eph 5:18-20).

Q. What should we ask of God in our prayers?

A. We should ask for everything that tends to the glory of God and to our own and our neighbor's welfare, both spiritual and bodily blessings.[4]

"Let the words of my mouth and the meditation of my heart / be acceptable to you, / O LORD, my rock and my redeemer" (Ps 19:14).

"Very truly, I tell you, if you ask anything of the Father in my name, he will give it to you" (John 16:23).

Q. What is the most excellent of all prayers?[5]

A. The most excellent of all prayers is the Lord's Prayer.

Q. Why is this the most excellent of prayers?

A. It is the most excellent of prayers because it is the prayer that Jesus taught his disciples.

Q. What is the Lord's Prayer?

A. It is as follows:

(Traditional)
Our Father, who art in heaven,
    hallowed be thy name.
    Thy kingdom come,
    thy will be done on earth as it is in heaven.
Give us this day our daily bread,
And forgive us our trespasses
    as we forgive those who trespass against us.
And lead us not into temptation,
    but deliver us from evil,
For thine is the kingdom, and the power, and the glory,
    forever. Amen.[6]

(Contemporary English)
Our Father in heaven,
hallowed be your Name,
your kingdom come,
your will be done,
on earth as in heaven.
Give us today our daily bread.
Forgive us our sins
as we forgive those who sin against us.
Save us from the time of trial,
and deliver us from evil.
For the kingdom, the power,
and the glory are yours,
now and forever. Amen.[7]

Other prayers helpful in this Christian life:

John Wesley's Covenant Prayer

I am no longer my own, but thine.
Put me to what thou wilt, rank me with whom thou wilt.
Put me to doing, put me to suffering.
Let me be employed by thee or laid aside for thee,
exalted for thee or brought low by thee.
Let me be full, let me be empty.
Let me have all things, let me have nothing.
I freely and heartily yield all things
to thy pleasure and disposal.
And now, O glorious and blessed God,
Father, Son, and Holy Spirit,
Thou art mine, and I am thine. So be it.
And the covenant which I have made on earth,
let it be ratified in heaven. Amen.[8]

The Collect

Almighty and everlasting God, to you all hearts are open, all desires known, and from you no secrets are hidden. Cleanse the thoughts of our hearts by the inspiration of your Holy Spirit, that we may perfectly love you, and worthily magnify your holy name, through Christ our Lord. Amen.

A Prayer of Richard Allen, AME Bishop, nineteenth century

We believe, O Lord,
That you have not abandoned us to the dim light of our own reason to conduct us to happiness,
but that you have revealed in Holy Scriptures whatever is necessary for us to believe and practice.
How noble and excellent are the precepts,
how sublime and enlightening the truth,
how persuasive and strong the motives,
how powerful the assistance of your holy religion.
Our delight shall be in your statutes, and we will not forget your Word. Amen.[9]

Trinitarian Prayer

Holy God,
you have given us grace,
by the confession of the faith of your holy church,
to acknowledge the mystery of the eternal Trinity
and, in the power of your divine majesty, to worship the Unity.
Keep us steadfast in this faith and worship,
And bring us at last to see in your eternal glory
One God, now and forever. Amen.[10]

A Prayer of Susanna Wesley

You, O Lord, have called us to watch and pray.

Therefore, whatever may be the sin against which we pray, make us careful to watch against it, and so have reason to expect that our prayers will be answered. In order to perform this duty aright, grant us grace to preserve a sober, equal temper, and sincerity to pray for your assistance.[11]

A Prayer Attributed to St. Francis

Lord, make us instruments of your peace. Where there is hatred, let us sow love; where there is injury, pardon, where there is discord, union, where there is doubt, faith; where there is despair, hope; where there is darkness, light; where there is sadness, joy. Grant that we may not so much seek to be consoled as to console, to be understood as to understand; to be loved as to love. For it is in giving that we receive; it is in pardoning that we are pardoned; and it is in dying that we are born to eternal life.[12]

In Your Own Words

1. Take some time and memorize the three rules: Do no harm. Do good. Attend upon the ordinances of God.

2. While some call these the "Three Simple Rules," they may not always be so simple to live out in our daily life. Talk about what these rules mean and share a time when you found it difficult to follow one or all of these rules.

3. Why do Christians need rules such as these? Or do they?

4. Share a time when God answered a prayer. Does God answer all prayers? How should we think about those prayers that God doesn't answer?

5. On a scale of one to ten (one being low and ten high), rate your prayer life this week. Does it enrich your life? Do you pray daily? Do you pray as a family? If so, when? What would you like others to know about prayer?

6. The disciples asked Jesus to teach them how to pray. What would you like to ask Jesus about prayer?

7. How is your soul? How can you point others to following Jesus in new ways?

8. Memorize one of the prayers in this chapter and pray it daily for two weeks. Then share what you experience with your group.

Conclusion

Embracing New Life

Imagine you are traveling to a new city for the first time. Within that city are places that you simply must see. There is a fabulous art museum, a restaurant that is famous for its local cuisine, a park with a statue marking an important historic event, a ballpark where all of the greats have played. Once you've explored the city and made it to these sites, you can really say you've been there, as opposed to someone who simply stopped at the airport while making a connection. Suppose, now, that as you explore this city, you realize that this is a city of such beauty, abundance, peace, and hope that you want to make your home there. Once you do so, you can sit in the art museum for hours on end and take in the beauty of the works. You can sample many different items on the menu in the restaurant. You can walk through the park and notice new things you never saw before, and you can see new, up-and-coming players, the greats of tomorrow, at the ballpark. No doubt, as you live in this city, you will discover new places you didn't know about before. You will get to know people and make friends. The longer you live in the city, the more chance you will have to get to know it, learn its secrets, and enjoy all that it has to offer.

Of course, even if you move to the city, none of this will happen if you sit in your house all day and watch television. You have to get

149

out and explore, avail yourself of the opportunities before you, go to the museums, walk along the trails, enjoy the local culture, and engage in conversations. The same is the case with the life of faith. Reading a book such as this one that walks through various topics of Christian thinking and living is rather like going on a guided tour. Guided tours can be useful, but a guided tour of a city will never teach you as much as living in the city itself. If you have not already, we invite you to accept faith in Jesus Christ as a kind of new spiritual home. This faith is one of beauty, abundance, peace, and hope. Visiting and learning about the major landmarks (as we have in the chapters of this book) are important, but if you really want to know this faith, you need to live there, and that involves a commitment to Jesus Christ and the ways in which faithful women and men have understood him through the centuries. Baptism is an important first step, but it is *only* a first step, for the life of faith goes on well beyond baptism. Baptism is how you move into the city, but what you do after that is up to you.

What we have provided in this book is only a beginning. The truths of our faith are far more complex, far richer and more filled with meaning, far more life-giving than we could ever explain in this book. In fact, we could write a book of ten times this size (as many people have), and still never fully express what it means to have new life in Jesus Christ. For good reasons, the truths of our faith have long been called *mysteries*. This does not mean that they are riddles to be solved, as one would solve the riddles of a Sherlock Holmes story. Rather, in this context mystery means a truth that is too profound for any person fully to understand. We can say that our God is the Holy Trinity, and in some ways we understand what that means, but the fullness of this truth is far too great for us truly to comprehend. We can say that Christ was fully divine and fully human, but exactly how that happens and what that means are, at some levels, beyond the ability of human beings to understand. These truths are mysteries, and we should expect nothing less from the eternal God. There is a legend about Saint Augustine, the fourth- and fifth-century Christian thinker, writer, and bishop. The legend goes that Augustine was walking along the sea, pondering the doctrine of the Trinity. As he did so, he came upon a young boy emptying water from the sea into a small hole with a seashell. Augustine asked what the boy was doing, and the boy replied that he was emptying the sea into that hole. Incredulous, Augustine asked the boy how he thought that he could get the entire sea into that small hole. In response, the boy asked Augustine how he thought he could understand the eternal God with his small mind. The boy, who was actually an angel, then disappeared.

We can know and love God. We can know certain truths about God, including that God knows and loves each one of us individually. Nevertheless, we can always grow in our faith, understanding, and love. Visiting the landmarks of the faith, then, is a beginning, and based upon that beginning, we can explore the faith more fully. How should we do this? There are many ways. We have talked about several in this book, the means of grace and ordinances of God. Growing from these practices involves a commitment to maintain a strong relationship with God, seek the guidance of the Holy Spirit, and contribute to the life of the Church. Being a Christian is about living into the mysteries of the faith, a process that takes place more and more fully over time. None of us will fully understand, for example, the mystery of the Trinity, but we can continue to live in the love and abiding presence of the Trinity, to accept the salvation that this God has offered to us, to pray that God will make us ever more faithful, and to engage in those practices such as prayer, worship, and communion that help us know God more fully.

When we begin to live into our faith, we also begin to see the world differently. We develop new perspectives regarding ourselves, other people, our vocations, relationships, and possessions. Life takes on new meaning, *fuller* meaning, rich with the possibilities of God's future. Creation has a purpose; life has a goal. In his book *Orthodoxy*, G. K. Chesterton discusses the type of person who has no room for mystery, whose universe is simply ordered by reason and materialism (belief in the physical world, but not the spiritual). "He understands everything," says Chesterton, "and everything does not seem worth understanding."[1] The Holy Trinity infuses the world around us with new meaning. We will find this meaning everywhere—in everyday conversations, acts of kindness, the six o'clock news, and, of course, in church. Reason and logic matter indeed, but mystery matters too. And we see the real possibilities of new life when we live into the mysteries of our faith.

There is no perfect church and no perfect theology. If you're looking for either one of these, you will be sorely disappointed. There is only the perfect God, the Father, Son, and Holy Spirit, who offers perfect love to imperfect people like each of us. Embrace the love that God offers you, and you will find new life now and forever.

Notes

Introduction

1. Unless otherwise indicated, all Scripture quotations are from the *New Revised Standard Version.*

2. "The Way to the Kingdom" in *John Wesley's Sermons: An Anthology*, eds. Albert C. Outler and Richard P. Heitzenrater (Nashville: Abingdon, 1991), 125.

3. *Roman Catechism*, Prologue, 10.

1. Who Is God the Father?

1. C. S. Lewis, *Mere Christianity*, revised and amplified version (San Francisco: HarperSanFrancisco, 2001), 162.

2. Ibid.

3. Ibid.

4. This statement comes from Article I of the "Articles of Religion" in *The Book of Discipline of The United Methodist Church* (Nashville: The United Methodist Publishing House, 2008), ¶103. We have changed "Holy Ghost" to "Holy Spirit."

5. This Q and A is taken from the *Eastern Orthodox Catechism* (Boston: The Albanian Orthodox Church in America, 1954), 16.

6. Ibid.

2. Who Is God the Son?

1. This Q & A is taken directly from "The Catechism" in *The Book of Common Prayer* (New York: Oxford University Press, 1990), 849.

2. Ibid.

3. Ibid., 850.

4. Answer adapted from Article XX of the "Articles of Religion," in *The Book of Discipline of The United Methodist Church* (Nashville: The United Methodist Publishing House, 2008).

5. Answer from the *BCP*, 850.

6. Ibid.

3. Who Is God the Holy Spirit?

1. "Come, Holy Ghost, Our Hearts Inspire," *The United Methodist Hymnal* (Nashville: The United Methodist Publishing House, 1989), 603.

2. The NIV reads, "and the Spirit of God was hovering over the waters." The NRSV translates this passage as "a wind from God swept over the face of the waters," offering in footnotes alternate translations of "while the spirit of God," or "while a mighty wind."

3. John Wesley, preface to "Explanatory Notes upon the Old Testament," in *Wesley's Notes on the Bible* (Grand Rapids: Francis Asbury, 1987), 20.

4. Many in the Western church, including leading Wesleyan theologians, believe that the phrase "and the Son" should be dropped.

5. Q & A adapted from Article III of the "Confession of Faith" in *The Book of Discipline of the United Methodist Church* (Nashville: The United Methodist Publishing House, 2008), ¶103.

6. Question taken from *The Book of Common Prayer* (New York: Oxford University Press, 1990), 852.

7. Ibid., 853.

8. We leave out "experience" here because it relates to the inner witness of the Holy Spirit, and to say that we understand the Spirit by the Spirit is circular.

4. What Are Human Beings?

1. See "The Image of God" in *John Wesley's Sermons: An Anthology*, eds. Albert C. Outler and Richard P. Heitzenrater (Nashville: Abingdon, 1991), 13.

2. Ibid., 14.

3. Ibid., 17.

4. John Wesley, "Thoughts Upon Slavery," in *The Works of John Wesley*, 3rd ed., vol. 11, ed. Thomas Jackson (Grand Rapids, Mich.: Baker, 1978), 76.

5. Ibid., 68.

6. This Q & A is taken from the *Book of Common Prayer* (New York: Oxford University Press, 1990), 845. The "Articles and Confession" say nothing directly about human nature.

7. *BCP*, 845.

8. Adapted from the "Articles of Religion," Article VIII, in *The Book of Discipline of The United Methodist Church* (Nashville: The United Methodist Publishing House, 2008), and *BCP*, 845.

9. Adapted from the "Confession of Faith," Article VII.

10. *BCP*, 845.

5. What Is Sin?

1. "Original Sin," in *John Wesley's Sermons: An Anthology*, eds. Albert C. Outler and Richard P. Heitzenrater (Nashville: Abingdon, 1991), 326.

2. Ibid.

3. Ibid.

4. Augustine, *Confessions*, trans. Henry Chadwick (Oxford: Oxford University Press, 1991), 1.1.1.

5. Augustine, *Confessions*, trans. R. S. Pine-Coffin (New York: Penguin, 1961), 4.12.

6. Q and A paraphrased from Luther's *Small Catechism* (St. Louis: Concordia, 1971), 92.

7. Ibid.

6. What Is Salvation?

1. Percy Livingstone Parker, ed., *The Journal of John Wesley* (Chicago: Moody Press, 1974), 378.

2. "The Scripture Way of Salvation," in *John Wesley's Sermons: An Anthology*, eds. Albert C. Outler and Richard P. Heitzenrater (Nashville: Abingdon, 1991), 372.

3. Ibid., 373.

4. Ibid., 373.

5. Edwin Hatch, "Breathe on Me, Breath of God," in *The United Methodist Hymnal* (Nashville: United Methodist Publishing House, 1989), 420.

6. See "The Scripture Way of Salvation," 3.9-10.

7. Eleonore Stump, "Atonement According to Aquinas," in Thomas V. Morris, ed., *Philosophy and the Christian Faith* (Notre Dame: University of Notre Dame Press, 1988), 66.

7. What Is the Church?

1. Samuel J. Stone, "The Church's One Foundation," in *The United Methodist Hymnal* (Nashville: The United Methodist Publishing House, 1989), 545.

2. John Wesley, "Thoughts Upon Methodism," in *The Works of John Wesley*, 3rd ed., vol. 13, ed. Thomas Jackson (Grand Rapids, Mich.: Baker, 1978), 258.

3. Taken from the "Confession of Faith," Article V in *The Book of Discipline of The United Methodist Church* (Nashville: The United Methodist Publishing House, 2008).

4. Q and A taken from the *The Book of Common Prayer* (New York: Oxford University Press, 1990), 854.

5. Taken from "Confession of Faith," Article V.

6. Q and A taken from the *BCP*, 854.

7. Ibid.

8. Ibid. This *catholic* is in distinction from the Roman Catholic Church, which is a particular communion within the catholic, or universal, Church.

9. Ibid.

10. This answer adapted from the *BCP*, 855.

8. What Are the Sacraments?

1. Introduction to "On the Duty of Constant Communion" in *John Wesley's Sermons: An Anthology*, eds. Albert C. Outler and Richard P. Heitzenrater (Nashville: Abingdon, 1991), 502.

2. "The Duty of Constant Communion," in ibid., 502.

3. Answer taken from the "Confession of Faith," Article VI in *The Book of Discipline of The United Methodist Church* (Nashville: The United Methodist Publishing House, 2008).

9. What Are the Bible and Creeds?

1. John Wesley, preface to "Explanatory Notes upon the Old Testament," in *Wesley's Notes on the Bible* (Grand Rapids, Mich.: Francis Asbury Press, 1987), 20.

2. Adapted from the *The Book of Common Prayer* (New York: Oxford University Press, 1990), 847.

3. Ibid.

4. Ibid.

5. Ibid.

6. Ibid, 848.

7. Ten Commandments adapted from Deuteronomy 5:6–21, *NRSV*.

8. Q and A adapted from the *BCP*, 851.

9. Ibid.

10. Ibid.

11. Ibid.

12. Answer adapted from the "Confession of Faith," Article IV in *The Book of Discipline of The United Methodist Church* (Nashville: The United Methodist Publishing House, 2008).

13. Taken from the *BCP*, 853.

14. *The United Methodist Hymnal* (Nashville: United Methodist Publishing House, 1989), 881.

15. Ibid., 880.

10. How Should Wesleyans Live?

1. See his book, *Three Simple Rules: A Wesleyan Way of Living* (Nashville: Abingdon, 2007).

2. "The Means of Grace," in *John Wesley's Sermons: An Anthology*, eds. Albert C. Outler and Richard P. Heitzenrater (Nashville: Abingdon, 1991), 160.

3. Richard J. Foster, *A Celebration of Discipline: The Path to Spiritual Growth*, 3rd ed. (San Francisco: HarperSanFrancisco, 1988).

4. Q and A taken from *Dr. Martin Luther's Small Catechism* (St. Louis: Concordia, 1943), 147.

5. Ibid., 151.

6. *The United Methodist Hymnal* (Nashville: The United Methodist Publishing House), 895.

7. This contemporary version of the Lord's Prayer taken from *The Book of*

Common Prayer (New York: Oxford University Press, 1990), 364. The prayer originates from Jesus' instructions in Matthew 6:9-13 and Luke 11:1-4.

8. "A Covenant Prayer in the Wesleyan Tradition," in *The United Methodist Hymnal* (Nashville: United Methodist Publishing House, 1989), 607.

9. *The United Methodist Book of Worship* (Nashville: The United Methodist Publishing House, 1992), 460.

10. *UM Hymnal,* 76.

11. *UM Book of Worship,* 528.

12. This version of the Prayer of St. Francis taken from the *BCP,* 833.

Conclusion

1. G. K. Chesterton, *Orthodoxy* (London: Bodley Head, 1957), 20.